# The Light

## A Modern-Day Journey for Peace

JUDITH T. LAMBERT

 ANN DURAN
PRODUCTIONS

Santa Fe, New Mexico

This book is dedicated to

*That*
Within and
Without
And to those
Who make it possible
To see

# Acknowledgments

The process of writing and publishing a book is a steady teacher. Of the many lessons I've learned, one is there are times you must rely on others for help. And in fact, many people have made this book possible. I would like to thank Nancy Palmer Jones for her unfailing editorial recommendations, manuscript preparation, and sincere guidance. For your support and assistance, a word of thanks to Crystal Jacobs, Helen Doust, Bill Roof, Colleen Lewis, Hank Rigler and David Tschanz. A toast to Johann Muller and Roy Gordet; you redefined the meaning of great penmanship in the academic sense. On the final lap, I am deeply indebted to Barbara Rainess and Jose Ramirez at Pedernales Publishing. To Barbara Ardinger, Ph.D., thank you for your editorial excellence.

Muhammad and Khulood, I will fondly remember our many conversations that brought about "A Niche for Light." Thank you for opening your hearts. And as with any creation of this nature, there are so many other people, friends and family, who as silent partners stood by me during this journey; I have often sought you for comfort and care, and I am truly appreciative.

Possibly from the inception of this work, its most significant advisor, both as a friend and guide through this maze, was Richard Kenyon. You believed in this project. "Thank you" doesn't seem enough for your unwavering encouragement. Finally, I am immeasurably grateful to the most important person in my life, my husband John. Without you, this book would not have been realized.

# Contents

The black moment is the moment
when the real message
of transformation is going to come.
At the darkest moment
comes the light.

— Joseph Campbell
*The Power of Myth* (1988)

# CHAPTER ONE

# Key to Global Spirituality

*I saw an intensely radiant Light*
*and I realized it was God.*

It's as if I have been propelled by an unknown force into the night sky. But what I see is not the night sky. There are no stars. Rather, it feels like I am floating, suspended in a cosmic, empty space. Although surrounded by darkness, I am not afraid. Without warning, as I lift my eyes, there appears a Light of intense brightness moving toward me. I am drawn irresistibly to it. Instantly it is near, and at once I experience an overpowering physical sensation of Love in my chest.

Absorbed in this feeling as I look at the Light, I suddenly realize I am looking at God. This revelation shakes me with new understanding, and I awaken with a start. I bolt straight up in bed, shocked back into the wide-awake daylight world. Yet the feeling within my chest continues—an intense feeling of Love beyond that known.

—My Dream

The redwood steps leading down to Rick's garden were slick from weeks of rain, and my heels skidded and almost slid out from under me, sending a miniature avalanche of gravel from the driveway down the steep slope and into the ferns. I grabbed at the sodden railing, stopped for a moment to stifle an impulse to swear, and then plunged forward against the slashing rain. Leaping from flagstone to flagstone across the sunken garden, I landed more often in the puddles. By the time I was halfway to the door, my jeans were clammy at the knees and clinging to my calves.

The front door opened, and Rick's face, looking as warm and relaxed as mine felt nipped and blanched, beamed out at me like a searchlight. "Wait," he said. "Don't move. I'll send out the ferry!"

I eyed the puddles in front of the wooden step that led to his door. "Oh, please!" I jumped the last two flag-stones in one stride, clutched his outstretched hand, and landed with a splash on the doorsill.

"Yes! You made it!" he crowed in the voice of an Outward Bound instructor. "A-plus for puddle jumping and stream fording for you, Miss! Now, on to rope climbing and vine clinging."

I rolled my eyes as I brushed past him into the hallway, where I shook off the hood of my rain jacket and began to pry my feet out of their muddy boots.

"No smile?" he asked. "Not even a flicker?" Without another word, he slid the navy blue jacket off my shoulders and disappeared with it down the hall. I knew he was going to hang it in the bathroom, one of the few places in his house where it could drip without ruining the hardwood floors.

When he returned, he was holding a pair of his own huge, brown-flecked wool socks. I leaned against the wall to strip off my soggy ones and roll his up under the wet legs of my jeans.

"Go sit by the fire," he said. "Can I get you a cup of coffee?" He had given up coffee eons ago, and his self-discipline while he indulged my habit baffled me. I managed a half-smile in acceptance and touched his arm lightly.

Rick's two-story cabin is nestled into a hillside in a stand of Northern California redwoods. Even on the darkest days, the main room has a copper-colored glow, its dark wood paneling reflecting the light of lamp and fire. Through the sliding glass doors that led onto the deck at the far side of the room, I could see the redwoods thrashing in the high wind. I perched on the edge of the couch close to the fire and felt the heat begin to warm the bottoms of my jeans. Steam arose from them. Rick's two cats lay in front of me on the hearth, curled around each other head to tail, a feline yin and yang.

I was still frowning into the flames when Rick came back, set a large mug of coffee on the side table, snuggled himself into a corner of the overstuffed sofa opposite mine, and picked up his mug of cooling tea. He waited. No more jokes or small talk. I glanced over at him, grateful, as I have been so often throughout our long friendship, for his willingness to read my moods…and bend to them.

When the logs crackled and spit, I frowned at the fire. My heart felt heavy and tight, as if a trap had snapped shut in my chest. I shook my head.

"Jude," he said, "what is it? Just start."

When I'd called him earlier that afternoon, I'd given

him no clue as to what was going on. "I need to see you," was all I'd said. That was enough. Now I looked at him almost apologetically and leaned back against the big pillows on the couch. "I have to start with the dreams."

"I love dreams."

"I know." I shook my head before trying again: "Okay, the first one was a couple of months ago."

Rick's eyebrows rose. It was unusual for me to have kept anything from him for that long.

"You'll see why I didn't tell you in a minute," I hurried on. That first dream had mirrored the classic near-death experience, the sort of thing people experience when a car falls on top of them while they're changing a tire. Such things, I firmly believed, did not and should not come to a person in the full bloom of health or in the innocence of a normal night's sleep. Yet my dream had been vivid, one of those from which you awaken feeling you've traveled a long distance.

"It began with some unknown force propelling me into the night sky," I said. "It was as though I were riding a huge, silent skyrocket on the Fourth of July. Only it didn't explode. And it wasn't the night sky because there were no stars. It was completely and utterly dark. I was just floating in a vast, empty space, suspended in the cosmos." I was almost whispering now. I squinted at Rick. He was squinting back at me, his head cocked, listening without judgment. Good, I thought, because there's more.

"It was surreally dark," I went on, "but I wasn't afraid." I was staring over Rick's left shoulder as though the dream were reeling itself out like a film on the wall behind his head. "Out of nowhere, an intense light appeared. It was moving toward me, and I was being drawn to it. In the next instant, it was as close as a breath, filling me with an overpowering sensation of love. Here, in my chest." I placed a palm there to show him. Just then I felt that snapped-shut trap inside me begin to open, just a little.

"I was totally caught up in this feeling of love, Rick, this warmth, a kind of peace beyond anything I've ever known," and I paused again, feeling the tension return. I groped for the words. "And then…well, I knew, I just knew, as I stared at this light that I was looking…at…at God."

Although I'd rehearsed these words during the drive over to Rick's house, I still couldn't say them without a tiny shrug and shake of my head. "Never thought you'd hear me say that, did you?"

"Wow."

"Yes, right. Wow," I agreed. "In fact, it was so shocking it woke me up. I literally bolted straight up in bed. My heart was pounding, but I still felt this incredible sense of love. I tried to just sit there holding onto it. Because in the midst of all this, I also felt this terror that the feeling would go away." I turned back to the fire.

"God." It wasn't an exclamation, nor did Rick sound sarcastic. He seemed to be tasting the word in his mouth for the first time. "God. Hmm." I watched him feel the sides of his mug for any remaining warmth, take a cautious sip, then grimace and reach out to set the mug down at the far end of the coffee table. But when he looked back up at me, his dark eyes were serious. "God…like, the Old Man? The guy with the beard?"

I had to stop and breathe for a moment. "No!" I

snapped. "Come on, Rick! Of course not! No. This God wasn't a person. Not a being at all. It was—what? It was The Light, Rick. *The Light* was God. It's not just any old light, it's *The* Light with a capital T."

"You 'saw the light,'" he half-murmured, but his sly grin disappeared as I leaned forward and waved my hand at him.

"Wait! That's what this means. I saw The Light!" And I flung myself back against the pillows. "This is the kind of thing that's been happening all the time. Ever since!"

"What; what? New insights into old clichés?" At his most skeptical, Rick could sound like his conservative, overly rational grandmother from Brooklyn.

"New insights into old everything." I thrust my chin forward in mock defiance, but then I wrapped an arm around one of the bright throw pillows beside me.

"Did you tell John you saw God?" he asked.

John, my husband, bless him, is rarely surprised by anything I tell him, even when I wake him in the middle of the night after I've dreamed of God. "John told me I should talk to you."

Rick leaned forward with his elbows on his knees and gave me his most intense investigative look. "Vell," he said in a sudden Freudian accent, "how very interesting zat you didn't. It hass been how many months zince you had zis dream, hmm?"

"Oh ..." I waved a hand vaguely in the air, but I couldn't just sit there under his gaze. I got up and circled the couch. The rain had not let up, and I put one palm against the sliding glass door for a minute to feel the cold before wheeling back toward the fire. As I made several of these small circuits, the cats woke up and watched me.

Finally I came to a halt at the back of the couch, pressed my fists into the rough upholstery, and leaned stiff-armed against it. "Something has me in its grip," I mumbled, my eyes down.

"What? What'd you say?" Rick's tone dropped into something gentler and more serious.

I looked up at him. "Something has ahold of me..." I tried to laugh, tried to say, "Phiff, such melodrama, spare me!" But when I opened my mouth, shaped for sarcasm, out came a hiccupping sob. "Darn it!" I dabbed furiously at the corners of my eyes with an index finger. "Darn."

Rick disappeared down the hallway and returned with a box of facial tissues. He half-sat on the back of the couch near me, his eyes cast down at his stocking feet, and waited while I blew my nose.

"You can see why I couldn't come right away," I muttered. And then it all tumbled out, those months after the dreams. Combing bookstores for books with the word "light" in the title. Glancing over my shoulder like a thief. Plucking out what I later learned to call the "classics" on near-death experiences: Raymond Moody's *Life After Life*, Melvin Morse and Paul Perry's *Closer to the Light*, and Betty Eadie's *Embraced by the Light*. Crouching on the store's carpeted floor, hiding the titles from other customers, skimming through the books and finding over and over that the descriptions of the near-death experiences, or NDEs, as the books called them, matched the pattern of my dream. Was I about to die?

"I walked around waiting for the other shoe to drop," I finally said. "Only I expected it to be a twelve-ton boot the size of Kentucky. I felt crazy, Rick. Paranoid." How could I verbalize this? "It was hard to go to sleep at night. Mostly, I stayed up until I was so exhausted I wondered if I had dreamt at all."

Rick reached across my tense back and massaged my shoulder.

Our eyes met.

"And then I had another one, anyway." I took a breath. "The second was even more shocking to me than the first: I was in our upstairs bedroom, and I'd been asleep, but I woke up suddenly, looked down at my hand, and saw that it had turned completely pink, and then I noticed that the color had seeped up my whole left arm. Again, I was filled with love. (Later I would write in my journal: 'Left arm = heart?') I rushed into the bathroom where John was shaving, and I showed him my arm. Then I ran out on the balcony, and as I looked across the stairwell, I noticed that a new room had been added and that an immense orb of beautiful Light was hanging there, speaking to me in a language I couldn't quite understand. There was no one particular image in the orb, but I knew that it contained many images. I fell to my knees in awe, worshiping this Light, and as the orb started to take off, I cried for it to return."

"Very Close Encounters," Rick proclaimed.

"Oh, I know! And I hated the idea of falling to my knees and worshipping something, anything, let alone a glowing orb!"

It wasn't that I didn't care or had never thought about matters of the spirit. For years, I had been seeking things that made me feel connected to something larger, a larger whole, perhaps. I'd found them in time spent outdoors:

long hikes in the mountains, walks on the beach, our yearly trips to the Sierra or beyond. I'd sensed them in the daily tasks of making a marriage work, of staying close to a small circle of friends. But going to church had never been a part of my life, and I certainly didn't know what "God" meant in that context. All I knew was that religions, mired in their own dogmas, too often seemed to make "God" small. They seemed to encourage a narrowness that could lead to prejudice, hatred, and war. I wanted expansiveness and peace. The idea of worshipping some figure or specific dogma bespoke a need to clutch at a straw in a river as wide as the sky. But whenever I tried to put words to any of this, my whole sense of connection to some indefinable something crumbled into dust.

Now my heart hurt like the muscle had been clenched for too long. Behind us, the logs popped like firecrackers. I jerked around to watch a few glowing embers strike the grate, wink, and die out. The cats twitched, and each one curled a paw over one ear.

"So," Rick said, "what happened next?"

"Well, this time when I woke up, still with that feeling of love, which left me almost gasping...this time I, I just wanted to get back to it. I tried to will myself back asleep, but I was wide awake. And then I began to wish I would die. As if that was the only way I could get back to that place of incredible peace." I had to stop for a minute. Finally, "And of course this freaked me out more than anything, wanting to die. I made myself get up and fix a really strong cup of coffee."

"Mmmm." Rick was eyeing my coffee. Now he seemed to be savoring the memory of that first sharp hit you get off the aroma alone. "Did that do the trick?" he went on, sounding wistful.

"No." I nudged his shoulder with mine. "No. I just felt more disturbed. So I went back to the bookstore as soon as it opened, but this time I bought the books and plunged in."

The reading had given me something to do, had given me a jeweler's loupe through which I could examine what was happening to me. This time, the differences between the near-death experiences and my own dreams were what struck me. How could I reconcile the difference between NDEs and my experience of being very much alive and seeing the Light? The descriptions in the books all seemed to focus on another world, on the afterlife, not this life, and they seemed to emphasize a separation of spirit from the material world. This ran counter not only to my natural instincts but to the feelings the dreams had left me. Besides, I was having these experiences while I was okay, not courting death or even a NDE. When I stopped to think about it, my experience had been of a very present, all-pervasive love. The vividness of the dreams and the fact that they were coming to me in the midst of my ordinary life, the feelings that hung around me like a vapor for hours afterward... none of these seemed to point at a different world at all. They were pointing at this very existence, to the here and now.

As I had these thoughts, I felt the same clutch of irritability that had gripped me as those days passed. *What nonsense*, the British headmistress who lives in my head seemed to snap. As though this troubled planet could be the residence of love. How New Age. How superficial. How silly.

"I thought all those people saw Jesus or something." Rick's skepticism interrupted my own. He crossed to the hearth and reached down to stroke the cats, who stretched under his touch. His tone was careful, but I knew this was an area full of land mines for him. In contrast to my liberal, outwardly-focused childhood, he had been brought up in a deeply fundamentalist family and had left the church, to his family's dismay, at age eighteen. One of the many things we had in common now was a deep cynicism about anything that smacked of "organized religion."

"Yep, it's true," I said. "Some of those authors say they're absolutely sure the Light is Jesus. But for others, the Light doesn't take the shape of a being at all. I guess that's closer to what I was seeing and feeling. I did read this great book by Philip Berman called *The Journey Home*, and he says..." I fished a scrap of paper out of my jeans pocket and read it aloud as I joined Rick by the fire. "'While the light is indeed universal and invariable in NDEs, we each bring to it our own set of cultural, religious, and personal expectations.' So I guess that's why we hear a lot about Jesus in this country. I guess people give the Light whatever name they already know. You see what I mean?"

Rick nodded. "Which is why it freaks you out to call it God."

I nodded.

"You don't want any of your coffee?" he suddenly asked.

"Oh, right." I sat down and took a sip, then went on. "So I started meditating again—"

"Good!" Rick interjected, so vehemently that we both had to laugh.

"Yes, 'good,'" I admitted. "But of course, now I've been meditating with a purpose, trying to will myself into having a vision of the Light again instead of just sitting."

He raised his eyebrows. "And has it worked?"

We'd had many talks over the years about how best to get wherever we wanted to go. Were we more successful when we set a goal and marshaled all our forces in a drive toward it? Or were we better off just noticing and listening and being with the problem?

"Of course it didn't work!" I lifted my mug in a toast to his told-you-so expression and took another sip. "But I did start to think that if this can happen to me without a physical or a psychic trauma going on, and without a strong religious background or focus, then maybe it's happening to a lot of people. Or has happened. In *The Journey Home*, Berman compares near-death experiences with the visions that religious mystics have. It's absolutely clear that people have been having these experiences for a long time. Maybe these days we're mostly hearing about NDEs rather than mystical visions because we're a more secular society, and we think religious 'adepts,' I guess you'd call them, are suspect. Well, we think they're crazy. Or at least, I do. And maybe it's also because we have the technology and the know-how to revive people who would have simply died. So we're hearing their stories more often."

Rick waited. "And?"

"Okay, I have this feeling, which I think is kind of weird. But these experiences aren't just near-death experiences, and they're not just limited to any one culture or tradition or to any one time or place. I have this feeling, and I can't shake it, that...well, this is bigger than that, much bigger than just a dream or two. And if I could just look into it, really dive in, then I could find the connections somewhere to something." My words petered out, and I shook my head again. What in the world was I even trying to say?

"Well, then," Rick's tone returned to the steadiness that I always found reassuring, "where do you start? How do you go about looking for these experiences?"

I grunted. "I don't know." I leaned back and looked at the waning fire. The logs were hissing and sighing, the flames now buried under a cloak of ash. Kneeling on the hearth, Rick reached for another log and wedged more kindling where the brightest embers shone. Both cats sat up and stared intently at the logs, as though willing them to ignite.

The fresh wood had just begun to snap when I tapped Rick on the shoulder. "You know what I need? A big library that houses books on ancient ideas and all kinds of esoteric literature from across the ages. Like the ancient Library of Alexandria!" I held both arms out to show how vast the collection would need to be. "Right? And then all I'd need would be a few hundred years to look and read!"

Rick smiled. "Well, you figure out how to get that, and I can guarantee you'll have an answer in your hands." We both laughed. "Hey, wait, you know what?" He was up and dusting off his knees. "I don't know if this is a lead or not but…I've got an old buddy of mine. He was my freshman-year roommate, actually, at Berkeley. He's a character. Still has the long hair and the Birkenstocks. Looks just the same as he did then, just a few more wrinkles." Rick's smile spread as he remembered: "He used to keep me up all night with these riffs on various philosophers. He was a humanities guy all the way while I was taking all the business courses. We don't see each other often anymore, but I like him. Anyway, he's been working for a library for a while now, in some big building downtown near the Civic Center. Have you ever been there?"

I shook my head.

"Go see this guy, Jude. He's really excited about what he does, and you never know what he's looked into. He's constantly reading. He always has a big fat book with him whenever I see him." Reaching into the drawer of the table beside the couch, Rick pulled out a notepad and then scribbled a name and number down, peeled off the top sheet, and handed it to me. "It's worth a try?"

"Sure. I guess." I squinted down at the paper. William Reinhold, it read, with the library's main information number.

"Hey, I'm starving." Rick slapped his knees, stood up and stretched as a flash of lightning and a house-rumbling clap of thunder erupted almost simultaneously. The cats scattered, racing down the hall toward the bedroom. Rick and I were startled, too, then looked across at each other with widened eyes and laughed.

"Well," he said, "I guess we're not going out. Can I interest you in the omelet du jour?"

I suddenly realized how hungry I was. I'd been living on cappuccinos for days. As Rick had already moved off toward the kitchen, I tucked the slip of paper away and ran to catch up with him. I laid my hand lightly on the spot between his shoulder blades—that oldest gesture of companionship between us—and we turned together to walk down the hall.

In the dark, without light,
I saw from my mind, from my heart.
I saw from the light in me, that is me.
It is not the object or the meaning applied by man,
but rather that radiant power within
that illuminates images into meaning
for all mankind.

— Anonymous

# CHAPTER TWO

# Symbols and the Radiant Power of Images

As far as we can discern,
the sole purpose of human existence
is to kindle a light in the darkness of mere being.

— Carl Jung
*Memories, Dreams, Reflections*
(1962)

"You go to the fifth floor. Walk around the atrium and go through the door marked Exit, then you'll be in a hallway, you see, and then you turn right past the ladies' room, and then you just keep turning right until you come to Language and Literature and you see the Staff Only sign."

The gray-haired volunteer at the library's information desk put down her book to trace a maze of circles and squares in the air with one index finger. It hung there long enough for her to focus dimly on it, and then, satisfied that it matched the map in her mind, she returned to her reading.

I repeated her words, "Language and Literature," over

and over as the elevator rose and deposited me on the fifth floor. I moved past the carrels and computer rooms and into the windowless hallway, turning and turning until I felt I'd circled back on myself. Finally, there was the staff-room door.

I knocked. I was looking down, wondering what the heck I was doing here, when it opened. I saw the Birkenstocks first. Birkenstocks with fuzzy socks. I looked up and was greeted by an angular face that offered a mixture of comfort and character, boldness and reserve.

"I'm Bill Reinhold," the man said, extending a hand. Although he was still half turned away and only glanced sideways from under one uplifted shaggy eyebrow, his blue eyes met mine with piercing directness. "Come in."

The room was surprisingly bright. I'd thought I had spiraled into the circular inner core of the building. A few old, gray, metal bookshelves met in one corner of the room, books laid there haphazardly, places marked by pink or blue request slips or yellow sticky notes. Two short cafeteria tables and a dozen bright plastic chairs were crammed in, and despite an open window, the room smelled strongly of very bad coffee plus a faint whiff of cigarettes.

"So you're a friend of Rick's," Bill said as we sat down. "It's been a long time since I've heard from that rascal. We were roommates in college, you know." He smiled at his hands, then clasped them over the potbelly that in middle age seems either to astonish or amuse those men who have been rail-thin all their lives. I imagined Bill as the type who would find this change fascinating, as though his expanding middle were an interesting and impersonal phenomenon to observe.

"So what did you want?"

His sudden, direct look almost made me gasp.

"Well, I am interested in...I've been looking...having...." Not sure what to say, I grasped the edge of the Formica table. When I looked up at him, his expression was patient and concerned. I started again: "I've been having some dreams with symbols that seem to be very powerful and consistent, and I'm wondering whether these symbols have a history or a larger meaning. Or whether other people—"

"Oh, yes, absolutely," he broke in. "All symbols have a history and a commonality. There's no question about that. Human nature demands that the abstract be expressed and confirmed in visible forms, so we create pictures of everything seen and unseen, known and unknown. The mind demands these images in order to grasp, verify, and have a relationship with all that cannot otherwise be perceived. Images are the means people must employ to understand ideas and feelings. Without them, we cannot reason. But," as I fidgeted a bit in my seat, he leaned forward and lowered his voice as if he wished to impart a great confidence, "but, you see, we often don't know where these symbols and images come from, do we? We forget their origin and the long history of their use, until we end by thinking that the symbol is the thing itself!" His eyes twinkled at me as if this were a great shared joke.

I smiled back at him, a little tentatively, and my eyes went to the vintage tie he was wearing. What had I gotten myself into? Was this man for real or just some kook from the '60s?

He must have read my mind because his face fell.

"Oh, I've plunged in, I'm sorry." He swam his fingers across the Formica as though smearing away an unwanted paragraph he'd scribbled there. "I'm sorry, I'm sorry. Favorite subject, don't get to talk about it often; let's start again. You were saying…something about your dreams?" And he looked so eager and apologetic that I suddenly felt I could tell him anything.

So I did. I told him all the dreams. There had been four or five by now. He listened, his eyes half-closed, his chin drooping and resting on his chest. He looked rather like a therapist at the end of a very long day. But as soon as I finished, he turned that piercing blue stare up toward the ceiling and seemed to study it, as though reading a heavenly inscription.

"Ever hear of Max Müller?"

I shook my head.

He twisted in his navy jacket, which seemed a size too small, then went on. "I'm not surprised. His theory was thoroughly discredited in the 20th century. They like to do that, you know, the academic community; they love to pooh-pooh what's new and different. Claimed he failed to supply adequate cross-cultural comparisons. Ha!" Bill looked at me to share his indignation, but, lost already, I could only shake my head again.

"Ah!" He slapped his forehead. "Start again; start again, William, slowly, slowly. All right, Miss…?"

"Just Jude," I replied.

"All right, Just Jude, if I understand you correctly, you would like to find other instances, across cultures and time, where light has been used as a symbol for the

Great Divine, and you wonder if others are still using this imagery today—"

"Yes!" I let out a sigh of relief.

"But what you don't realize," he laid a narrow finger alongside the tip of his nose, "what you don't quite yet see is that you are surrounded by images that all point to Light. Now the question is…do they or do they not also point ultimately to God? Hmm?" And before I could reply, he'd pushed his chair back and was making his way to the door. "Come with me!" he called over his shoulder as he opened the door. I grabbed my backpack and notebook and followed him.

Bill led me back out through the fifth-floor maze and down multiple floors. We finally arrived in an area that managed to seem old and dank. As we wound our way past shelf after shelf of books, he picked up the thread of his earlier thought and explained that Max Müller had been an anthropologist who had raised many of the questions I was beginning to ask. Müller had tried to prove that all religious names and symbols ultimately personified the sun. Even though he had a large grassroots following and a groundswell of interest, his theory was discredited.

"Typical," Bill muttered.

But by this time, we were at the end of a long, dark hallway, and he was unlocking a door that I expected would squeal when it swung open.

It did squeal, and we stepped into a tiny room into which had been jammed a huge, old, oak desk with a computer on it and two swiveling, green-backed secretary's chairs. Every other available inch of the room was occupied by books. They were crammed into the shelves, stacked on the floor, lined up along the sill of a high window that otherwise would have looked out on the sidewalk and provided some light for the wilting purple azalea in the midst of the clutter. This was Bill's private lair.

He flicked on the desk lamp, swung the seat of one chair in my direction, and immediately began pulling books from the shelves and building a leaning tower on the desk. And all the while he kept on about Müller.

"I'm convinced that if he were alive today," he said, opening each book to ensure it was the one he wanted and then shutting it with a snap and adding it to the pile, "he would have sufficient evidence to support his assertions and silence his critics. At least as far as the cross-cultural comparisons go. With today's technology—mmm, yes." He turned to his computer and leaned down to start it. "Boot up the beast..."

He gave me a sharp look. "Be forewarned," he said. "You must realize that poking about among symbols threatens their meaning and value—their very existence—and that these are held dear by different factions in different ways. People use symbols to understand the world, but they don't necessarily like to think about how those symbols work. It makes them uncomfortable, and people hate to be uncomfortable." He sat down so abruptly the chair gave a little bounce as he swiveled it toward the computer. "Now, what's the first symbol for light?"

"The first?" Was this a pop quiz? Fire? Lampposts and light bulbs? Flashlights? Auras? All these ideas trooped through my mind.

I squirmed, then said, "Weren't we just talking about Müller?" If a British headmistress held court in my brain, inside Bill's must have sat a first-grade teacher.

Suddenly the glowing orb from my second dream reappeared before my mind's eye, slowly spinning and murmuring, and I felt the now-familiar grasp and clutch in my heart. I shook my head to rattle the memory away. "The...sun?"

"Yes! The sun, the sun!" Bill cried. "You know, of course, about sun worshippers, and I'm not talking about the tanning freaks in Hawaii. I'm talking whole cultures that were convinced that the sun was the One True God. Like Sol Invictus of ancient Rome and the Mithra cult. I'm talking kings and queens assigning it to themselves as a kind of pedigree. They proclaimed themselves Sons of the Sun...well, Sons and Daughters of the Sun. That's what 'Inca' means: Son of the Sun. Did you know that?" Bill barely glanced at me as he asked the question and didn't pause long enough for me to look up from my notebook. He was tapping away at his keyboard, drumming his thumbs on the desk as he waited for a new screen to appear, fluttering his fingers over the images, seeking words, phrases, paragraphs to copy and save in a new file. And all the while his own words kept tumbling out.

"Nearly every royal household has made the association, *Le Roi Soleil*, Louis XIV, being the most obvious example. The sun, of course, the source of our light. Everyone wants a piece of that, you bet. But that's on the crudest level, hardly counts as symbology at all because it's so easy, so what else? What else?" Suddenly he was leaning across the desk in my direction. "What other symbols for light?"

"Well, let's see, the sun...so there's sunshine...rays of the sun, um..." I felt like a stumped *Wheel of Fortune* contestant. I tried again. "The golden rays—"

"That's it! That's it! You've got it! *Gold*. From the earliest eras of human history, gold was valued as the metal of the sun, so it has an obvious link to the light. All cultures have viewed gold as representing light and wisdom. Gold is the metal of perfection, the color of the gods." He shot me a look to see if I appreciated this brief poetic flight. "Ah, and indeed, here we go," he went on as the computer flashed a new page on the screen. "*Oro*," he read, "Latin for 'gold,' ultimately, comes from Sanskrit, where it means 'the high one.'"

He nodded. "So there you are, not even three degrees of separation. It's not just gold—sun—light—God. But the link between gold and God was at some point a direct one. Hmmm."

Feeling overwhelmed (already), I put my pen down and slumped in my chair. "I'm lost, what does this have to do with me," I wanted to say, like a frustrated six-year-old.

Bill noticed. "Oops, you're losin' 'em, William, you're losin' 'em! Back up, back up!" He flung himself back in his chair, as if taking his own chastisement literally.

Then he launched into a vivid description, part personal reminiscence, part academic treatise, of churches, temples, mosques, synagogues all studded with gold, from external architectural features, such as spires and inlaid scrolls, to the sacramental objects within...the chalices, tabernacles, reliquaries, host carriers, candle-sticks, icons, and "don't forget, the Ark of the Covenant."

He was touching down, all too briefly, in worlds I had never seen, never cared to explore. But now something began to stretch in me, like one of Rick's cats, and I felt my curiosity, or was it wanderlust, starting to stir.

"But don't you see," he interrupted his own stream of consciousness, "in the modern-day world, we're used to thinking of gold in a strictly monetary way, for its material value. Certainly it makes sense to use the most precious stuff of this world in churches and temples as a way of honoring what we hold most high. It's a kind of payment, a sacrifice of our most valued worldly goods. And so on. But...but if gold actually means 'the high one,' then it becomes more than just 'valuable stuff.' It becomes a symbol for the very stuff God is made of!"

"No, wait," I said. "Now you're talking about *worshipping* gold? 'Filthy lucre'?"

Bill's laugh surprised me as it seemed to fill the tiny room like a genie. "That's good, that's good," he sighed at last. "But you're not thinking in symbolic terms yet, you see. This is where you're stuck." He ran his finger down the spines of the books piled on the desk till he rapped one right in the middle. "Here, could you—?" I stood up to clutch the top half of the stack while he wiggled the book he wanted out and flipped it open to a colored plate. He turned the book so it was facing me. "Now what do you see?"

A team of white horses pulling a golden chariot on which blazed an image of the sun. The picture brought back vague memories of junior high school and Edith Hamilton's *Mythology.*

"Keep in mind," he said, "that the horse was sometimes a sacred image, too. Often sacrificed to the sun."

I winced and he nodded.

"Yes, those were bloody days." He paused for a millisecond, then plunged on. "But here, notice the color, white. Quick—what comes to mind!"

"Uh, weddings, rice, snow, ermine, eggs, halos."

"Yes, yes, good. But right away when you see it, you should also be thinking: *light!* The presence of all the colors in the spectrum. Remember that. Better still, think symbols. Now, if the Light is pure and clean, then white is its natural reflection. Unblemished, uncontaminated, unspotted. The white wedding gown, the gowns of ermine worn by royalty, the white robes of religious figures, "Knights in White Satin"—"

"—and God's beard," I interjected wryly.

"Even that." He smiled and winked. "Especially that. All the major religions have used white in this way and so have societies at large. Sometimes, oh, yes, the imagery has been used in a racist way...you know, as though we white people are pure, and darkness is ignorance. Ha!" His laugh erupted again, and he spat out, "Nonsense!" With his index finger he traced the spiraling trajectory of an imaginary arrow, an arrow driving straight for my forehead. "Now, you, Jude," he said in a kind voice, "from now on, you will remember to look for the origin and symbolic meaning of white whenever you see it."

"Okay." I turned back to the picture in the book. "So,

white horse, golden chariot, the sun and its rays…all of them sacred symbols, yes?"

"Better yet, all of them images of light. *Gold, white,* and the *sun.* Think of them like arrows, pointing this way, this way," he jabbed his finger through the air. "Once you crack the code, you're going to find these used everywhere and from now on you're going to know what they mean."

And then he launched into a long riff, referring occasionally to the computer file of phrases he had printed out for me, but mostly improvising on the origins and uses of symbols for light: the circle, the eye, the mirror, stars and obelisks, even the lotus as a symbol of creation and the sun. Paging through the book, he found a picture of King Tut emerging from a lotus. "Our material being emerging from the Light, perhaps," he tossed out, and then he plunged on.

My hand was tired now, my handwriting illegible. He had shed his too-tight jacket and at one point he propped his feet on the desk. When he finally put them down again and smoothed his brown tweed pants, the riff came to an end and he was quiet for a whole minute.

"When you know the history of these symbols," he said quietly, his hands clasped again over the bulge of his belly, "then their real function becomes clear. You've got to continually remind yourself that the picture is always just the vehicle to guide you to a higher meaning. All of life, all of our physical existence, is emblematic. Do you see?" This time, his bright blue gaze held a wistful longing.

To tell the truth, I wasn't sure I did see. We'd traveled a long way from my dreams, and Bill's assurance alone that so many symbols were originally created to point us humans toward the Light seemed too easy. Too pat. Where was the evidence now? Why would we have so thoroughly forgotten these deeper meanings? And would I ever return to that feeling of peace and love that the experience of the Light had given me?

When I found my way back to street level, it was already dusk. From the sidewalk, I could identify Bill's window by the dim light of the lamp still burning behind his tower of books.

\*  \*  \*

"It's your golden opportunity," John said as he sipped the last of a glass of wine. "If you'll just follow the Golden Rule."

"If I just don't lay a golden egg," I shot back. All through dinner, we'd been improvising our own riff, finding the symbols Bill had listed in everything from advertisements to movies and mottoes. From the Oscars to the Olympics, the golden arches of McDonald's to the golden mean. We couldn't stop topping each other.

After all the serious and still-unanswered questions of the last few weeks, our silliness was a relief, and John seemed to offer me the game as a gift. As the coup de grâce, he whipped out a dollar bill, looked closely at it, and feigned surprise. "Look, darling! It's a sign!" And he pointed to the rays of light streaming from the top of the pyramid.

We laughed, but I felt the fist in my chest tighten its grip for a moment. I savored the last of my wine and stood up, leaning across the leftovers till I could grab his hands holding the dollar bill like a flag ready for folding, so I could reach his lips with mine.

...and he looked and behold,
the bush burned with fire,
and the bush was not consumed.
And Moses said, "I will now turn aside,
and see this great sight,
why the bush is not burnt."

— Moses at the Burning Bush
Exodus 3:2-3
*King James Version*

# CHAPTER THREE

# Masters of the Light

May the father live
In his aspect of the light
Which is *in* the sun-disk

— Akhenaten, King of Egypt
Ruled 1353–1336, BCE

I leaned my head against the curved corner of the airplane window and tugged at the thin blue rectangle the flight attendant had generously called a blanket. While it covered my shoulders, it left my shins and feet out in the chilled, recycled air. I'd asked for an extra blanket, but the attendant had made no promises before she'd turned away. Now I could hear her several rows down, regaling three businessmen with tales of near misses over the Cairo airport. The mere mention of the name Cairo excited me with visions from the *Thousand and One Nights* and excitement to come.

It would have been impossible to sleep anyway. I felt a sharp pang of longing for John's presence beside me. He would have been doing imitations of the passengers and crew that would have left me sputtering with laughter. Or if Rick had just said yes when I'd asked him to join me, right now he would have been murmuring an analysis of the psyche of the passenger in Seat B-17 and describing his favorite song. But when the opportunity arose for this trip to Egypt, both John and Rick had said, "Go," and "Go alone."

The speed with which it had come together seemed amazing. And auspicious. A few days after my meeting with Bill, I'd been pawing through the red and yellow bell peppers at the co-op market when I'd felt a quick touch on my arm.

"Jude?" It was my old friend Gail, whom I hadn't seen in at least seven or eight months. "I was just thinking about you!" she crooned as we hugged.

"Really?"

"Yes! It's the funniest thing. A tour to Egypt came up on the computer this morning, and I suddenly had the clearest picture of you standing in front of the Pyramids—now, don't laugh," she grinned, knowing full well that all this sounded like a classic sales hype. Gail had left the book club where we had met when her travel agency had begun to flounder and demanded all her time and energy. Now she looked refreshed, successful, and sincere. "I'm serious," she assured me. "There you were, standing on the edge of the desert, dwarfed by the Great Pyramid of Cheops and just flooded with light."

*What?*

"And get this," she went on. "From all around the very tippy top of the pyramid these bright sun rays fanned out, you know, like an optical illusion? I know," she held up a hand to forestall my interruption, then went on in a conspiratorial whisper, "but trust me, I was wide awake and stone, cold sober, and I'm simply not...psychic."

It was true. Gail's comments on the books the club had read, from James Joyce to Franz Kafka, had always had a practical, down-to-earth quality, as though she planned to use them as how-to guides for setting up a small business or constructing a new home. Her acute sense of humor about herself had saved her from seeming downright dopey.

Now she dimpled and went on: "So I think you've got to go, don't you? Besides, it's the most incredible deal. If I thought my hair would survive the heat, I'd go myself."

And she laid out the whole package for me, right there next to the organic produce. I could barely take it in. First, I was distracted by that vision of me standing at the base of the Pyramid. Second, I remembered the image of the dollar bill stretched out flat in John's hand a few nights before. Dazed, I simply laughed, gave Gail another hug, tucked her business card into my purse, and turned my shopping cart toward the checkout line.

When I got home, the message light was blinking on the machine. "Miss, oh, sorry, sorry. Jude," it was Bill's voice. "I've rediscovered the most extraordinary thing. A wonderful guidebook, if you will, for this journey you're undertaking. Most provocative. Another discounted theory, of course...I think you'll—Sorry?" The voice paused. Was he waiting for me to say something? Had he forgotten he was leaving a message? Was someone talking to him? "Oh, sorry, sorry. *Focus*, William," he began again just as abruptly. "Someone's at the door, you see—yes, yes, come in, come in!" I pictured the visitor standing on the threshold of Bill's lair, backlit by the hallway fluorescents. "So," he rushed on, speaking to me again, "I'll leave it for you at the front desk. Um, in your name. Jude. Oh, and do send me a card; let me know what you find! Now, my friend, what can I do for you?" He had launched into the next conversation before the phone had hit its cradle.

Send him a card? It did seem strange: Gail's offer of the tour, then Bill's mention of my "journey," both within an hour of each other. My intuition began to sing, "Go!" So when John and Rick, my two closest confidants, sang an echoing chorus, well, here I was, somewhere over the Atlantic, with a too-short blanket and a wildly racing mind.

"'Focus, William,'" I muttered to myself, as I pulled out the book Bill had left for me: a slim old hardbound copy of *Moses and Monotheism* by Sigmund Freud. Gail had sent me off with plenty of guidebooks, but I would indeed need something extraordinary to lead me where I really wanted to go. All the more extraordinary, because I hadn't a clue where that place might be.

\* \* \*

I began to read in earnest despite the fact that most of my generation had discredited Freud long ago. Bill had said to read it. So read it I would in belief that Bill's insight wouldn't lead me astray. Freud's thesis was alarming, or at least I could imagine how alarming, even offensive, it would have been to someone steeped in traditional Western religious thinking, especially at the time the work was written in the late 1930s. Freud proposed that Moses was born an Egyptian and was not a Hebrew child found among the bulrushes and brought up by Egyptians. What's more, Freud claimed that the whole religion Moses handed down to the people he led out of Egypt derived from the Egyptian king the historians call the "first monotheist," Akhenaten. Jewish theology, Freud said, was a direct descendant of Akhenaten's insistence on the omnipotence of the one god, Aten.

Moses, according to Freud, was either a member of Akhenaten's royal household or a loyal governor of a border province who took passionately to this new religion. When Akhenaten died, and the deposed priests of the old religion reinstated the old pantheon, Moses chose to leave Egypt. And so he found a group of oppressed Hebrews and led them out of Egypt where they could follow the new faith.

The details of the story didn't interest me so much; besides, Bill had included in the package he'd left for me a concise summary of the points critics had lobbed at Freud's argument. They were many and convincing. Even some recent archaeological research seemed to prove, for instance, that Moses and Akhenaten could not possibly have lived at the same time. But none of this diminished my fascination with the way Freud built his case and the "history of God" he had laid out. From the sun-god, Aten, of Akhenaten to the fiery Yahweh, of Moses, it was all a synthesis that became the One God of the Jews. Freud spun a lively tale of conviction, courage, ambition, political unrest, escape, rebellion, murder, conversion, remorse, negotiation, and union (or reunion). And he cast all of this myth-making within the context of his psychological theories.

It was a short book, so I had time on the long flight to read the whole thing and then go back to the parts that intrigued me most. A picture began to build in my mind's eye of the two men, Akhenaten and Moses. Akhenaten: brave, profoundly devoted, overthrowing Egyptian polytheism's emphasis on numerous gods. His was a very here-and-now religion, I imagined, something like the feeling my dreams had given me. "He recognized in the energy of the sun's radiation the source of all life," Freud wrote, his own admiration unmistakable, "and worshipped the sun as the symbol of his God's power." I felt like Bill was sitting beside me, muttering, "Ah-hmp. The sun—a sacred symbol—and an image of…well, the source of light."

My pulse quickened as I turned back to Freud's depiction of the pharaoh.

Akhenaten himself was a pacifist, as was his god, but the pharaoh had faced plenty of political turmoil. All those disgruntled priests who felt he'd usurped their place had made quite a stink, and as the priests' resistance mounted, Akhenaten's prohibition of temples and wor-ship services other than those focused on Aten had grown sterner and more exacting. He had even ordered all the inscriptions on the old monuments changed to blot out the word "god" when it appeared in the plural. When the political climate grew too hot for him to stay in Thebes, he built a whole new capital at El Amarna, where all the art and temples and inscriptions could be focused on the Aten.

And then there was Moses. In Freud's version, a talented, ambitious man, a man of passion and action, a loyal follower of the religion of Aten who refused to set his beliefs aside when the political tide turned against Akhenaten. Instead, Moses gathered a group of "strangers" and marshaled them out of the country and into a new life governed by the law of the One God. Even sterner and more exacting than the pharaoh, Moses also made enemies and met with resistance from the people.

Two men, both flying in the face of social, religious, and political pressure, passionately committed to the One Universal God. What had given them such courage and conviction? And why had their ideas not met with wider acceptance? Indeed, why had their beliefs stirred up such violent antagonism?

One of Freud's sentences echoed over and over in my head: "Religious intolerance...was inevitably born with the belief in one God." In all my years of avoiding organized religion, I had sensed that any claim that there was only "one way" to believe was divisive and that it was an illusion as well. Better to forgo them all than to be trapped in rigid doctrine that judged others so frightfully. If I took Freud seriously, were Akhenaten and Moses to blame for all the religious strife that had torn peoples, nations, and the world apart for millennia?

Something was dissatisfying in the thought. It seemed too simplistic. But the stories of Akhenaten and Moses stirred my imagination in a way I couldn't dismiss. I was on fire from thinking about them, and I kept wondering why Freud was so insistent that they had known each other. Was that enough or even necessary? Was it presumptuous for me to think Freud hadn't adequately spelled it all out in his profound little book? And did I honestly think I could challenge Freud's hypothesis? That would be swimming in turbulent water. And yet, I kept asking myself if there wasn't a clear, tangible, visible and obvious connection between them that one could *see*. Was there something Freud had overlooked? It was on the tip of my tongue, but I couldn't put it to words, so what was it? Compelled to set off on my own adventure, I guess I felt a kind of sympathy for Moses' and Akhenaten's obsessions. They had become my own.

I shook my head and tucked the blanket around my knees. Such vague thoughts and feelings. Ever since my experience of the Light with its overwhelming sense of certainty and love, I'd seemed to be groping my way along a dark corridor, anxious and unsure, aching for a return to that bright sensation of all-encompassing peace.

I pulled out the notebook I'd used in my interview with Bill and turned to a blank page. Bill had been right in at least one sense. Freud's book was a kind of guide, for it had given me a new sense of purpose. My first project when I landed in Cairo would be to follow in the footsteps of Akhenaten and Moses and look for some clue that might lead me out of this tunnel and into the Light.

\* \* \*

The package Gail had sold me included my choice of several tours of Cairo and the surrounding countryside. For my first full day in the city, I picked "Rediscovering Moses," even though I thought the title and the description full of exclamation marks were corny. The brochure promised that the tour would lead me "back to where the story began!"

This seemed as good a place as any to start.

Early the next morning, thirty pilgrims from all around the globe boarded the bus in Tahir Square. I sat in the front, where I could get the first glimpse of the sights through the bus's curved windshield and where I would be as isolated as possible from the other tourists. Last to board was our guide, a trim young woman with gleaming black hair pulled tightly back in a ponytail. She introduced herself as Huda and immediately launched into a rote overview of the tour we were taking. She sounded a lot like the brochure copy, only stripped of the exclamation marks. My heart sank.

Huda retold Moses' story, the traditional (not the Freudian) version, as the bus stopped and started through Cairo's busy downtown streets. Finally we reached our first destination: one of three locations claiming to be the "original spot" where Moses had been found among the bulrushes. Claimant No. 1 was in the basement of the ancient Ben Ezra Synagogue. The Nile had "changed course," the ever-neutral Huda explained. *I'll say it did*, I thought.

The queue of tourists snaked into the bowels of the synagogue, following a roped-off path. Once inside the dim room, the line slowed to a shuffle as each visitor stopped to examine the identified hallowed spot, some of them kneeling to get closer to the floor, as though they were archaeologists with a thrilling new find. Others were merely paying respect. While I was waiting, my gaze wandered around the room. All the trappings of what must be in a synagogue still in use lined the walls: stacks of dark books, long folding tables, low bookshelves on which some glossy books lay sideways, some rough wooden crates overflowing with items of probable religious significance, a row of bright posters written in Hebrew. "A lighted vessel," I murmured aloud, for in the center of each poster was a symbol, a Chanukah menorah. I was surrounded by symbols of light.

"Excuse me," the elderly woman behind me said sharply. I turned to explain, but she scowled and gestured me forward. I was holding up the line.

The object of such fascination for my fellow tour members was a dark brass plaque, in Hebrew, with a printed English translation posted nearby. Exodus 2:1–10, the "beautiful baby" in the willow basket, among the reeds on the bank of the Nile.

I felt let down. I could have stayed in California if all there was, was a quotation from the Bible.

Glancing back at the posters, I nearly ran right into Huda. She was studying a sheaf of notes, but she looked up at me, then over my shoulder at the posters, as I moved past her into the glare of the sun.

"Claimant No. 2," Huda began when we were on the bus again. She described its claim to legitimacy as we drove on. Her monotone never varied. She sounded like she had been programmed. I wondered why the tour managers hadn't simply recorded an audiotape the driver could play.

At the second site there was at least water to support the story that this was where Moses had been found. Huda pointed to a spot in the middle of the Nile River, right in the heart of downtown Cairo, "It was there," she said solemnly.

I rolled my eyes.

Soon the driver maneuvered the bus into a narrow turnout lane. This was to be a longer stop with time to visit the shops that lined the riverbank and the vendors offering overcooked native fast foods like shish kebab and falafel. Our little colony of tourists scuttled off the bus, the others chattering among themselves, snapping pictures of each other wearing broad smiles and pointing, as Huda had, toward the center of the Nile. They seemed eager, even hopeful. The more bright-eyed they became, the more my irritation grew. I was the last to get off the bus.

I took my turn noting the spot from the shore, then found a place where I could lean against the cement retaining wall and watch the Nile ripple past. I was making no progress. All this tour was revealing was that no one really knew where, or if, Moses had been "found." It was all a myth, anyway, I thought, as I lifted the bottle of water I'd bought and drank it quickly.

"Is bad for you to drink so fast." Huda's low voice suddenly broke into my thoughts. I turned and involuntarily frowned. My response seemed to make her almost cringe. "Oh, pardon me." She was quiet for a moment, then she went on, "I have noticed…" Huda's eyes posed the question as they met mine. "You do not like the tour?"

Something in her tone slipped past my irritation and exhaustion—the cumulative effects of jet lag, frustration, and the commercialization of the tour.

"No," I said. "I admit, I am not always the biggest fan of tours, especially when I'm tired." I gave her a wry smile.

"Yes, I agree," she said simply. And then she offered her own story. A Coptic Christian, she was currently enrolled at the university and earning a doctorate in religious studies. When her funds ran low, she'd taken the one job she could find, a tour guide, despite the fact that the tour promoters had no deep understanding or respect for the traditions they were exploiting. Our eyes met for a prolonged moment. But as I was about to speak, the bus driver honked. It was time to board the bus.

The last stop, the third claimant for the bulrushes story, took us out to Memphis and Saqqarra, the ancient capital, some fifteen miles south of the Great Pyramid. This time I lingered in order to fall in step with Huda, and I ventured to tell her of my interest in Freud's book. Her eyes danced at the mention, and she launched into a rapid-fire analysis of the strengths, weaknesses, and implications of his theories.

We rounded a curve and I turned around to see the Great Pyramid rising on the horizon with the afternoon sun setting behind it. The dusty air split the sun's rays into a hundred sparkling shafts.

"Let me take you to El Amarna." Huda was staring at me with the same intensity I'd now noticed several times.

"But how? Do you have time?" I half turned to her, expecting some catch or hesitation.

"Yes, yes, Miss, I need to go."

My pulse quickened at the urgency in her voice. I'd felt the same way when I first went to Rick and told him about my dreams.

"If you will pay for our transportation and lodging," Huda was saying, "I will offer you in return all that I have learned. This area of Egyptology is my passion, but I could never afford to travel there. Few tourists venture to that part of Upper Egypt and even fewer have any historical background like you do."

By the time we were back on the bus, we had made

our plans, and I'd promised Huda that I would stop at the bookstore she recommended and buy the books that would tell me more about Akhenaten.

Perhaps I did not "rediscover Moses," at least, not that first day. But the tour had led me to Huda, and she might lead me...where? We would see.

I slept soundly that night between the crisp white hotel sheets. No dreams at all.

*   *   *

The five-hour drive south along the Nile and deep into our quest had been exhausting, but I was now sitting in the courtyard at the front of the hotel, refreshed and waiting to have lunch with Huda. The noon call to prayer was beckoning the men to come to the mosque. I opened one of the books on Akhenaten. What struck me most was the strength of his conviction. It showed remarkable bravado to insist on a monotheistic creed centered on the sun. Why would he do this? What had inspired him?

I turned to the slick colored plates at the heart of the book. There was a picture of the symbol Akhenaten had chosen for his God; a solar disk whose rays terminated in tiny hands that stretched toward the earth, hands often holding *ankhs*, the ancient Egyptian symbol of life.[1]

"Ah, you found it." Huda was suddenly beside me,

---

1    In the manner of John Anthony West, I would like to propose a symbolist interpretation for the Egyptian ankh. I suggest it is an *inverted* yoni/lingam originally adapted perhaps from Vedic tradition. Scholars already recognize the ankh as representing the uniting of both cosmic and physical energies of male and female in the formation of physical being, or life itself.

also staring down at the image. "But you must understand, Akhenaten would never have permitted, how do you say, a graven image, to be made of God. This symbol was that alone. A symbol designed to point to a force greater than all." Her words echoed Freud's.

Huda had explained to me what was known, what was surmised, and what was forever lost about Akhenaten's religion: the dismissal of all other priests, the building of the new capital at El Amarna, the belief in a life of truth and justice. At the dismantling of his empire by invaders, Akhenaten stood fast to his pacifist principles. But Huda's impassioned monologue and the desert heat were causing me to fade out. We settled on a light lunch and agreed to reconvene the next day.

In order to avoid the oppressive midday heat, our private tour began early the next morning. The city of El Amarna was built on a low plateau along the east bank of the Nile. It was more or less an easy walk from one part of each excavated site to another. But Huda and I lingered over every feature, with Huda offering commentary to accompany the translations of the posted signs. This was an inspirational tour. This was enlightenment. The sun, meanwhile, seemed to climb not higher but closer. Each new angle gave off a more intense heat than the last. Sweat had already made a sticky band around the crown of my hat. Still we strolled on, the hot dust of the paths coating our sandaled feet. Huda was reciting Akhenaten's hymns, which stressed the loving-kindness of God and invited believers to wonder at the beauties of nature. The latter was a doctrine I could espouse; though I would have given much for a very different natural setting, a cool shaded forest path, say, and a brisk mountain stream in which to dangle my feet. My focus was beginning to waver like a mirage, and my body grew heavier and heavier in the heat.

Finally we arrived at a rock tomb. Huda stood silent for a moment before the hieroglyphics.

"This is Akhenaten's prayer," she whispered, "his 'Hymn to the Sun.' Here," she took my hand and placed it gently on the inscription. Standing close, she guided my fingers over the hieroglyphics as she murmured a translation:

> May the father live
> rejoicing in the horizon
> in his aspect of the light,
> who is *in* the sun disk,
> who lives forever and ever.

Despite the fact we were now out of the direct sun, heat radiated off the relief, bathing my face, arms, body, and shimmering in the air around me so brightly it was hard to see. I closed my eyes and felt the rough stone under my fingers, the deep crevices of the strange figures.

"The light which is in the Aten," Huda went on, "the light which is God."

I swayed and clutched at the wall, and then everything vanished, and I was floating in an all-embracing light, completely at ease, filled with love.

"Jude!"

Huda's hand on my shoulder woke me. She was

leaning down. I had sunk to the ground, and she was offering me a bottle of water.

I returned, hearing the murmurs of tourists gathered in a curious but respectful circle, to Huda's admonitions that I should "drink much water, slowly, slowly," and to the blazing sun, now partly blocked by the wall at my back.

Heat stroke? What had happened? Why were these people staring at me? Embarrassed, I leapt to a new conclusion. Perhaps my dreams were nothing but physical imbalance. The irritation cleared my head.

"Let's go," I said brusquely as I struggled to my feet.

Only much later, alone in my hotel room, did I remember something Freud had written, something that Huda also had mentioned. Akhenaten wasn't worshipping the sun itself. No, of course not. The sun was a convenient and familiar image on which he could hang his much larger belief that the light was God beyond form and being.

The magic of the trip to Upper Egypt and Huda's insight had opened the door to the beginning of understanding.

And suddenly I knew, beyond the shadow of a doubt, that Akhenaten had also had a direct experience of the Light. Perhaps it was in a vision or a dream, or perhaps he had engaged in some rigorous spiritual practice now lost to us. But this was the only possible explanation for what some had come to call his fanaticism. He had had an encounter with the Light, and he had felt compelled to pass along this new awareness to everyone around him. Akhenaten's Aten wasn't just a commonplace picture of the sun. Akhenaten used it as a symbol to teach about the Light!

I felt such an enormous relief that I wanted to call home and tell John what I had discovered. But I stopped with my hand on the phone. *Wait*, I counseled myself. *This is only the tip of the iceberg—the tip of the pyramid.* I pulled the special dollar from my pocket and remembered another time. I was smiling as I fell asleep.

\*   \*   \*

I knew I was being followed, but it hardly mattered, as I was so preoccupied and absorbed in my own thoughts. Hoping to cool off, I'd gone to the Egyptian Museum, a semi-air-conditioned haven in the middle of Cairo. If I'd hoped for a break from my search, however, I'd come to the wrong place. Everywhere I looked, the artifacts spoke the language of symbols Bill had taught me to read. White alabaster cups, vases, and *canopic jars*. The gilded royal chair emblazoned with a shining disk; golden goddesses safeguarding golden mortuary chests; a golden mirror in the shape of an ankh. The golden death mask of King Tut. Item after item spoke of the Light.

Freud believed King Tutankhamen, next on the throne, was Akhenaten's son-in-law. Other books had thought maybe Tut had been his nephew. But I had also read somewhere before my trip that DNA testing confirmed the Boy King was Akhenaten's son! That's what mattered in my mind. Here was Amarna art staring back at me from the reaches of time. Hardly a degree of difference! All the golden treasures of Tutankhamen's tomb showed that the principle of the Divine Light had not died with King Tut's father.

I arrived at the museum just toward closing, so it was practically deserted when I reached the jewelry room at the back of the massive building. The shadow that had pursued me at a distance from the front rooms now edged closer. This time I turned quickly and saw the braided trim at the hem of the guard's *djellaba*. He was standing just outside the room I was in.

"Excuse me," I said loudly as I walked toward him. My heart was beating faster. Was he going to attack me back here in the lonely reaches of the museum? My eyes scanned for a doorway that might lead to a closet or a stairwell, but saw none. And then, just as I whirled to plant myself accusingly before him, I saw his eyes light up and a broad, innocent grin spread over his face. He made a low bow and beckoned me toward the largest of the cases in the middle of the room. Beneath the glass gleamed a row of golden necklaces. The guard pointed to the heaviest of them and, in an elaborate pantomime indicated that he would like to take it out for me and let me try it on.

"What?!" I gasped, almost laughing incredulously. He stood still, his eyes cast down. "Ahh," I added, "for a price, you mean!" His eyes and lips flicked upward in an eager smile, then down again.

I looked back over my shoulder and saw that we were alone. "All right." I took a deep breath. "Let's do it."

I was drawing a crumpled bill from my backpack when the guard, even more excited than I was, brushed past me to the case, slid an ancient looking key into the lock, and lifted the glass lid with one hand. With the other, he drew the necklace out in a gesture both tender and familiar, then let the lid close with a slight clink. Cradling the necklace in his two palms, he nodded to me to turn so that he could fasten it around my neck.

My heart was racing now, but I turned and lifted my hair. The heavy gold settled against my skin and sent a chill through my body. The guard stepped back and applauded silently, then grew solemn and bowed to me. Breathless and giddy, I went to an ornate mirror on one wall and saw the glow that the gold cast across my neck and chest.

The emblems of the necklace leapt into focus: a *scarab*, gods and goddesses with the solar disk on their heads, a baboon, a falcon, a serpent, and a lotus. Bill's lessons had been thorough, for I remembered that all these images pointed toward a greater idea: the principle of the Light. Tutankhamen also had recognized the Light as the supreme power of the universe and had left the encrypted message that was crying out to me now.

I managed a dazed smile as the guard snapped a picture of me in the sacred regalia. After another minute; he slid the necklace from around my throat, replaced it in the case. I glided back through to the museum's front rooms, as silent as he had been throughout our encounter.

\* \* \*

My room, a short distance from Mount Sinai, held just a thin mattress, a shaded lantern, and an old Bible. But I was grateful for the simplicity. I had chosen a two-day bus tour, leaving Cairo and driving east to the Suez Canal before hugging the coast of the Sinai Peninsula and down to St. Catherine's Monastery.

"Here Moses parted the Red Sea," my new guide, a pale young man named Arik, said in a bland voice. "This is the first stop on 'The Path Moses Trod.'" Yes, I was trying again for a Moses sighting. "You may disembark for the taking of photos and the purchasing of gifts."

All I saw were a paved parking lot and vendors selling baseball caps labeled "Red Sea."

We drove on, and some hours later Arik said, "Here people worshipped the golden calf." Around me camera shutters clicked. "Here Moses struck the rock, and the water sprang forth." More clicking of cameras, and, sure enough, the vendors at this stop were selling plastic bottles filled with the sacred liquid.

By the time we reached the monastic-looking hostel near the base of Mount Sinai, my internal British headmistress had launched into a harangue of her own. *You stupid, stupid girl,* she chided me. *You are wasting your time and mine! Now get to work!*

I had just a few hours before a monk would collect our little group to make the predawn pilgrimage to the summit. Anxious and wide awake, I picked up the Bible and turned to Exodus. The story of the baby found among the bulrushes brought back images of Huda and El Amarna and my new and dizzying belief that Akhenaten had "seen the Light." I skimmed ahead to Moses' encounter with the burning bush. With my finger marking the place, I imagined Moses' first glimpse of God in a burning bush that was not consumed. He had spoken with a God whose only name was "I am that I am" and whose property was light.

The posters on the walls of the old synagogue I'd visited flickered before my mind's eye. *Menorahs*, lamps and candles, the same imagery still fed the Jewish faith. And then there was the *Kabbalah*...wasn't the *Ein Sof*, which is located at the top of the mystical Tree of Life, the Infinite Light? Was this how and where Judaism absorbed the light of Moses, and was Kabbalah a direct link from the Israelites' remarkable encounters?

I thumbed through Exodus, the chapters describing the fire that guided the Israelites by night, and the brilliant glory that filled the tabernacle. Wasn't the *Shekinah* glory the visible manifestation of God that resided with the Ark of the Covenant? I imagined the black tents huddled together on the desolate plain, the wanderers suddenly awakened by an extraordinary light that hovered over the tent they had designated as holy. Did it fill them with fear, or reassurance, for their journey into the unknown?

And then I came to Exodus 34:29–35:

> As he came down from the mountain, Moses did
> not know that the skin of his face shone because
> he had been talking with God. When Aaron and
> all the Israelites saw Moses, the skin of his face
> was shining, and they were afraid to come near
> him. But Moses called to them...and Moses spoke
> with them.... When Moses had finished speaking
> with them, he put a veil on his face; but whenever
> Moses went in before the Lord to speak with him,
> he would take the veil off, until he came out; and

*when he came out, …the Israelites would see the*
*face of Moses, that the skin of his face was shining;*
*and Moses would put the veil on his face again.*

Something spacious seemed to be opening up inside me. I stepped carefully through my thoughts, as though I were back among the artifacts at El Amarna. Moses glowed so brightly from his encounter that he had to veil himself or his people would be frightened. If that was so, then maybe Moses had returned from a long and intimate contact with the Light. In fact, it seemed to me that perhaps he had almost ingested it, and that had affected the very cells of his body, transforming him into a being of light which shown back for all to see. Moses was shining.

The epiphany held me. It didn't matter whether Moses had known Akhenaten or not or whether Freud's whole argument could hold water or not, for now I had my own theory. It didn't matter what their religions said or didn't say; did or didn't do. Akhenaten and Moses had daylight encounters with the Light and probably dreams of it, too! These two men had been compelled by the same vision. Each had had a direct experience with the Light. This was their binding agreement. Moses, realizing that Akhenaten's symbol of the solar-Aten was still confusing, decided to use only Light itself as divine. That was it! That was where the two great leaders met. They were both Masters of the Light!

Exhausted from the mental puzzle I had pieced together, I lay back on my cot and stretched. Pulling my coat over my legs as a blanket, I hoped I might finally be able to doze off. But as soon as I closed my eyes, a now-familiar question repeated itself over and over: how was I to find this Light? Would it flood me with the rising sun on the summit of Mount Sinai?

I could hear footsteps approaching along the stones of the cloistered walkway. Wrapping my coat more tightly around me, I slipped out into the darkness.

Religion is a candle inside a multicolored lantern.
Everyone looks through a particular color,
but the candle is always there.

— Mohammed Naguib
First President of Egypt
1901–1984

# CHAPTER FOUR

# Islam and a Niche for Light

If light is in your heart,
you will find your way home.

— Rumi
Persian Mystic and Poet
1207–1273

The sunrise on Mount Sinai, for all the buildup, had seemed, well, pretty ordinary. Maybe it was the distracting presence of all the other tourists, or maybe there was just something lacking in me. After all, visions appeared to the extraordinarily devout, to pharaohs and heroic leaders. Why in the world should I think they would come to me? Had my dreams been a fluke? I reminded myself that I was traveling in uncharted metaphysical territory.

Suddenly the whole trip seemed foolish. There were still six days before my return flight. Nothing left but to hang out in Cairo, an ordinary tourist, missing John and feeling adrift.

Just a few blocks from my hotel ran a walkway along

the Nile. I thought I could disappear among the tourists there. The river was a well-traveled highway in which single-sailed narrow boats that my guidebooks identified as *feluccas* sailed. I wished I were on one of them. Sailing had been my father's great passion. He used to take me out on San Francisco Bay on Sundays, all-day outings, just the two of us. I would hear him call to me early in the morning. "Jude? Let's go to church!" It was our private joke, as my father had not been inside a church, except for weddings and funerals, since his childhood. Even so, the rituals of preparing the boat to cast off had had a sacred quality.

"Missus! Missus!" A boy's voice broke into my thoughts. No more than nine or ten years old, he bounded up to me, his brown eyes wide and eager. "You want ride on boat, Missus? I give you ride, all day, very beautiful, lunch on river, you will like, yes, Missus?"

I couldn't help but smile back at his insistent cheer-fulness. Someone must have told him that Americans smile a lot. "You have your own boat?" I asked. He seemed too small for such a large possession.

The boy nodded, smiling even more broadly.

"How much?" I rubbed my fingers together in the international symbol for cash.

The boy named a figure that would have bought me my own boat, and we set about haggling like merchants in the *souk* until finally he brought the price down to something close to what my guidebooks said to expect. The boy seemed as pleased as I was and led me to his felucca.

But when we got there, I found the boat already occupied. A stately man rose from one of the cushions, stepped out of the boat, and spoke sternly in Arabic to the boy. The boy replied rapidly, his arms gesturing widely, his bare feet dancing on the dock.

I watched the man begin to smile in spite of himself until finally he threw back his head and laughed out loud. Then he turned to me and spoke in an accent that mixed England and the Middle East. "This young entrepreneur," he clapped a hand on the boy's shoulder, "promised me a ride in his felucca. No sooner had I boarded than he claimed that he had to go to market for some food to eat on our excursion. But do I see his arms laden with fruit and bread? No! Instead he has brought you!" He shook the boy slightly in mock disapproval, then looked back at me, smiling warmly.

"I'm sorry…if you'd rather travel alone…" I started to turn back.

"No, no," the man said. "Please, no, that is not it at all, I was simply marveling at the business acumen of our young friend here. He'll be wealthy before he's twelve." He gave one last gentle shake to the boy's shoulder, then turned his full attention to me. "Please allow me to introduce myself. I am Dr. Muhammad Najjar. From Damascus. I would be most honored to share this felucca with you." He made a slight bow and offered a hand to help me into the boat.

I'd pictured myself sailing silent and alone except for the boy. But now Dr. Najjar's outstretched hand and calm, inviting manner promised a pleasant distraction from my solitude. I took his hand and stepped in, introducing myself as we settled ourselves on the cushions in the middle of the boat.

We sat quietly for a while, watching while the boy cast off and, with sharp cries to his fellow boatmen, maneuver our slim vessel away from the cluster of boats at the dock. Once we were in the clear, the breeze filled the sail and moved us steadily up the river. Now the only sounds in our little world were the gentle lapping of water along the sides of the felucca and a low humming from the boy, absorbed in his task of navigating the Nile.

From the banks of the river came the early morning sounds of the unloading of trucks and the grinding of gears mixed with the rattle of carts and clopping of donkeys' hooves as they headed for market. The city was a cacophony of the ancient and the new, of luxury and squalor. I looked across at our barefoot and bedraggled captain, as comfortable as a king and seemingly oblivious of his two passengers now that his daily income was assured.

I caught Muhammad's eye and nodded toward the boy. He smiled back at me. "Ah, yes, the look of a great man." And then we began to talk. He told me that he had been invited to Cairo to speak at a conference on population growth sponsored by the Arab League. I also learned that he had earned his doctorate at Cambridge and had spent several years working in London before returning to Syria. He also confessed that though he had been to New York, he had always wanted to visit California.

"And what brings you to Cairo?" he asked as he turned to me.

I laughed a little as I answered, "Oh, I'm just searching for the meaning of life, the universe, and everything."

"Ah, then you need look no further." And his gaze grew more intent. "The truth has been revealed to us all."

"Oh, really? And I suppose you know this truth?"

He nodded slowly and solemnly, and then his smile broke through, and we both laughed.

"Please call me Muhammad," he said, "and please allow me to clarify," he began again, his tone lighter and more fatherly this time. "I am speaking of Islam." He added that Islam is the ultimate revelation of God for more than a billion people around the world. "I believe, as do all Muslims," he said, "that God's message is succinctly summarized in the Qur'an, which God dictated to the Prophet Muhammad, peace be upon him, through an angel." His voice caressed the last word. "The Angel Gabriel."

I'd taken one course in college, eons ago, on the history of world religions. A bit of what I'd learned came back to me now, and I replied, showing off, I suppose, for my new companion by reciting the five pillars of Islam: the declaration of belief in one God and in the role of Muhammad as the messenger of Allah; the practice of prayer five times a day; the requirement that one fast during the holy month of Ramadan; the importance of giving to the poor; the encouragement to travel to Mecca, if one possibly could, to perform the *Hajj*. I was proud of my memory.

"Very good," Muhammad cocked a most approving eye at me. "Those are our basic laws. But Islam is so much more than a legal code." He pressed his lips together briefly, narrowing his eyes and then turned back to me as though he had decided to take a chance. "Tell me, do you know what a Sufi is?"

"Ah," I hesitated, wanting to show off for him again. But then I had to admit my ignorance. "Not really."

"It's no wonder," he hastened to reassure me. "Only a few pursue the mystical in Islam. No matter what the sect, *Sunni* or *Shi'a*, some will choose the path of esoteric knowledge, the inner hidden meaning of Islam. And these are the people called Sufis. Their perception of God…"

"Would be…?" I prompted.

He seemed to be sizing me up for a moment, so I looked steadily back at him. Flecks of white-hot sunlight reflected off his dark eyes, just as they did off the rippling surface of the river. I felt surrounded by jewels.

"*Allah* is the Light of the heavens and of the earth." He gazed past me as he quoted,

> *The similitude of his light is, as it were, a niche wherein is a lamp: the lamp within a glass: the glass as it were a pearly star. From a tree right blessed is it lit, an olive tree neither of the East nor of the West, the oil whereof were well-nigh luminous though fire touched it not: light upon Light!*

"Do you know what this means?" he asked.

I could only shake my head. Here was the Light again!

"This is the passage from the Qur'an called the Light Verses," he said. "To me it holds the key to Islam's ultimate beliefs. It is much more than ordinary poetry, you see. We believe this is reality." Again his gaze held me. "Does this interest you?" Unable to find the words to express just how interested I was, I put my hand to my heart.

"Well, then," and he smiled again, "I would be happy

to offer my personal insights into how these verses inspire the devout."

I settled back against the cushions, my own smile reflecting the pleasure that suffused my whole being. What a curious turn the day was taking. I was more relaxed than I'd been in weeks. Muhammad leaned forward, and as his voice rolled over me, a little murmur in my head repeated, *The similitude of his light is, as it were, a niche wherein is a lamp: the lamp within a glass: the glass as it were a pearly star.* Muhammad's words echoed as he continued, "You see how everything is connected—light within and yet ever surrounded by light? Allah is the Light that burns without burning up."

"Like Moses and the burning bush?"

"Ahh, Musa'a. A great prophet, a messenger, so too the Qur'an records it. A man who beheld God. Just so, the ultimate goal of every Sufi is to behold the pure Light that is God. Our whole lives consist of a process designed to elevate our souls to union with the Divine Light."

I could hardly breathe. "How is that possible?" I whispered.

"Ah, well, this goal requires a great deal of work and dedication." He shrugged his shoulders as if to admit that sometimes his own dedication flagged. "But we have extraordinary teachings about it. I'm particularly fond of one, *The Niche for Lights*, by Abu Hamid Muhammad al-Ghazzali, a great mind and someone who was acutely devout. Al-Ghazzali, you see, was a distinguished professor until he realized that he could not *think* his way to God. He had to seek out the experience of the Most High about which he spoke. So he, too, became a Sufi, and it is to him that we owe the acceptance, even now it is rare sometimes, of how dedication to the *Shari'a*, to the law, must be intricately interwoven with the mysteries of faith."

Muhammad suddenly lifted his hands and face skyward. "*Alhamdulillah,* praise be to God, and so Sufism, too often misunderstood, has flourished." He beamed at me, as though this were his own personal success. "But about the Light. Sufis experience Allah first as the sun, then as the Light of Lights, then as the Pure Light Itself. But don't let yourself be confused with these varieties. Simply remember that the light you see here in this world, our physical light, is merely a metaphor for the supreme luminescence."

The sun as "merely a metaphor." That made me think of Akhenaten and his solar disk's tiny hands stretching toward Earth. Now this man I'd met "by accident" was also speaking of symbols. "Think of them like arrows," Bill had said about the tiny hands, "pointing, this way, this way."

"Allah," Muhammad raised an index finger to emphasize his point, "God is not only the source of all the light you see, but He is the only real Light in existence."

"The source of all the light we see," I repeated. "Isn't that like the Big Bang theory?" Silly as this sounded even to myself, I was happy to have something to contribute to the conversation. "Or even the creation story in the Hebrew Bible, you know..." My voice trailed.

"Hmm, perhaps, perhaps." He sat back for a minute to admire the scenery along the shore. Life was still bustling, and the scenes of early morning marketing met our eyes and ears. I was feeling disappointed. I wanted to impress my new friend, but he was hard to read. Should I tell him about my own experiences with the Light?

But before I could form the words, he began again. "Sufis learn special techniques so that they can enter into a mystical union with God. With the Light."

I sat forward.

"Ah, that interests you." His look was appraising again.

"Interests me very much," I admitted. "How does one learn these techniques? And are women allowed to learn them?"

"Well, you understand, in my country, women are..." Watching for my reaction, he shrugged, his tone almost apologetic. Then he quickly grew serious as my face showed some of my irritation. "I assure you, there have been women who have practiced these techniques. I will tell you sometime about our famous Rabi'a al-'Adawiyya, from the eighth century, whose love for Allah was a light to all who saw or heard of her. And there are women now. Anyone may learn these techniques, anyone, that is, who is willing to prepare the heart to receive the Light. But to be so willing is very rare. And," he cautioned, "you must have a guide. Someone who knows the way and is spiritually elevated."

"A guide?"

"Yes, indeed. And eventually, when one is fully prepared to achieve self-realization, he, or she,"—he almost winked at me—"goes into seclusion for forty days. I cannot tell you the whole story, you understand. These rites are for initiates only. But I will tell you that when we do our chanting and our whirling rituals, this is what we are striving for, both individually and as a community. We are seeking this union with the Light that is Allah. You may have noticed that we twirl with one hand pointed up and the other down." He made the gesture. "The hand pointing upward is extended to receive the Light, and the other passes the Light on to earthly life."

"That's beautiful."

"Ahh, but it is even more resplendent than that." He voice grew warmer as he spoke. "We enter wearing a black over-robe, which is removed just before the whirling to reveal our radiant white robe beneath the dark robe. White for purity and light, as God's Light is pure. The dark robes symbolize where we are presently in the world. The white, where we are going. For instance, on pilgrimage in the holy city of Mecca, we wear white as we walk around and around the *Ka'bah*, which is draped in black."

Here he noticed that I was lost, and so he stopped to explain. "The Ka'bah is that Holy of Holies we call the 'House of Allah' within Mecca's great mosque in Saudi Arabia. It is toward the Ka'bah that we pray five times each day. Embedded in the southeastern corner of the Ka'bah is the Black Stone, kissed by the *hajji*, the pilgrims. We believe that this holy spot was established by Isma'il. Do you remember the story of Ishmael, Abraham's rejected son, from your Bible?"

"No, not really," I had to admit. "My biblical history needs work. But please go on."

"The father of my people," he said. "Well, we pilgrims wear white to show that we are leaving our darkness behind. The Ka'bah is draped in black because the God-head is a mystery and is veiled from our vision. But," now he leaned forward so that we were closer together as he gave a revelation. "Beneath this black draping are exquisite golden doors. The golden doors of heaven. Although not readily revealed, they are there for those who search."

A large tourist boat pulled past us, suddenly casting its shadow over us, Then it plowed on and left our little felucca bobbling in its wake. I grabbed the sides of the boat, but Muhammad simply sat back.

"Now, Sufism," his tone was suddenly precise, "categorizes people into various levels according to the amount of light they hold within."

*Oh, God,* I thought, *is he wondering where I belong?* "Are we aware of our personal place in this hierarchy?" I asked, my voice suddenly small.

Muhammad grinned.

"Oh, all right, you got me!" I admitted. "I need to know where I stand!"

He laughed with me. "Do not worry, my friend. Sometimes you know your place. But mostly you are not made aware until you have reached the higher levels." He paused for a moment, as though taking stock of his own level of awareness, and when he went on, he spoke with a longing that echoed in my own heart. "Souls are graded reflections of the Divine Light. There are no less than seventy thousand veils that keep us away from the final realization. The highest soul is like the image of the sun in a mirror. But that soul is neither sun nor mirror. At that moment, we are one with the unveiled sun, the unadulterated Light itself."

We were staring at each other. Then squealing tires and the crunch of a car colliding with a fruit wagon jolted me back to the chaotic life onshore. The car was cocked at a crazy angle across the road, the cart upturned, and fruit strewn across the pavement. The drivers stood face-to-face, outraged, their arms flailing.

Muhammad and I looked back at each other, but the intimate spell of a moment before was broken.

"Two souls still lost in darkness," he assessed with a nod at the arguing men.

"A few more than two!" I had to raise my voice to be heard over the din, for behind the drivers cars had quickly backed up, and the air was now filled with honking horns and shouted insults. Somehow this struck us both as funny. The release was a relief and we laughed until our eyes were wet.

"Okay." Muhammad wiped his eyes with a large white handkerchief and grinned at me. "We have not finished our lesson in Sufism yet, my friend. Do not think you can distract me."

I grinned back at him.

"So, here is something you must know. The essence of Islamic mysticism, according to this practitioner, at least, can be found in the single word, *ishraq*."

"Ishraq," I repeated dutifully, as though uttering it would reveal its meaning.

"Ishraq means 'illumination,'" he said. "It is much the same as your word 'enlightenment.' You see how both these words embody the image of the Divine Light?"

"En-light-en-ment." I tasted each syllable. "Yes, of course. It does capture the flooding in of light, doesn't it?"

"You know," he hesitated, for what he was about to say would sound like criticism, "most Westerners understand Islam only in a very theoretical way, if at all. With all the animosity between East and West looming in our consciousness, weren't you afraid to come here? And come here alone? You are very brave. Or, my dear, are you perhaps driven?" He held me in his gaze. There was a momentary pause. "You see, the experience of Allah has been misunderstood, and mostly ignored, in your world. But it is just this experiential involvement with Allah that is the driving force behind Islamic spirituality. Of course it is important for us to study the law and theology, and we have an extensive philosophy, but the highest value is always placed on experiencing the divine through prayer. That is one of the reasons why we pray five times a day."

Maybe that was what I needed: a prayer practice. But how was I to leap into something so new and foreign? Even my best efforts at meditation hadn't been what I would call successful.

\*    \*    \*

Our young Egyptian captain suddenly called out in Arabic, breaking our discourse and pointing toward the shore and an outdoor café where tourists and Egyptians all crowded the small square tables. I could hear Egyptian music coming from a too-small cassette player, and the aroma of grilled kebabs sparked my appetite.

"Lunch here," our young captain announced as he docked the boat. "*Itfaddal, itfaddal...* Welcome, welcome." He jumped out, tied up the boat, and led us up the ramp to the tables, each decorated with a single plastic rose in a small blue hand-blown vase.

"Speaking of prayer," Muhammad murmured. He had his small prayer rug rolled up under his arm. He walked around the side of the café and joined a group of men, bowing and kneeling on their rugs. I watched, thinking how this was a very masculine activity in this part of the world…and then I suddenly wished I could see Muhammad whirling in his Sufi robes. The fantasy surprised me and I turned back toward the Nile.

The waiter followed Muhammad back to our table and laid down a small paper tablecloth and set our silverware on it. Muhammad ordered the drinks in Arabic. We would dine from a set menu of local specialties. Over lunch, he began to teach me Arabic phrases, beginning with the names of the dishes as they arrived. "This is *shiish tawooq*, grilled chicken."

"*Shish tawuck*," I tried.

"*Shi-ish ta-wooq*," he corrected, grinning. "And *tabbouleh*, but you must know that. Lots of parsley, yes? *Hummus*, of course, made from chickpeas. And, ah, the staple of the Arab world, *khubz arabii*"—he shook a slice of it in the air—"our pancake-shaped bread. *Sahtain!*" he said as he dove in, and then, at my puzzled look, he added, "That means 'enjoy!'" In his intonation, it sounded like the most personal of invitations.

While we feasted, he pointed out the major landmarks on the horizon, coaching me in the correct pronunciation of the names of the mosques we could see from our table. I struggled to wrap my lips and tongue around the unfamiliar syllables and saw that my new friend's eyes were twinkling.

"You are actually trying to wipe that smile off your face with your napkin, aren't you!" I accused him. And we laughed again.

"No, no, you are doing so well," he assured me. "So much better than most of your countrymen. Who would not even try," he added.

Now we were interrupted by the sound of a ferry returning from a morning trip to the city, its decks packed with shoppers.

"Huh," Muhammad grunted, and once again there was a bitter edge to his tone. "They do not know that they are trapped."

"Trapped? On the boat?" I joked.

But he ignored me. "Do you know about the Night Journey of the Prophet Muhammad, peace be upon him?" he asked. His voice rolled toward me, spinning a haunting tale. "*Al-isra* and *al-mir'aj* tell of the Night Journey and the Ascent. These stories flow one from the other. The Prophet was brought to Jerusalem and from there rose through the seven heavens and to the very throne of Allah. There, he saw oceans of light. He heard what ears had never heard, saw what eyes had never seen, and learned what had never penetrated the heart of humankind. He grasped what we are all here to learn." He paused, his voice a focused whisper, "That only God is the Truth."

"What does that mean to you, Muhammad?" I asked gently.

"That we become confused and entrapped by the things of this world and think they are superior to God. This becomes the great test for us. We must prove that we love God over and above everything else." His voice was confident and secure. "Without being tested, how can we prove our worthiness? There is only one purpose to life, and that is to know yourself. If you know yourself, then you know God. If you know God, you yourself become divine."

He sat back and for the first time that day, his eyes seemed clouded. The effect on me was of the sun slipping irretrievably behind a cloud. I even shivered. He reached for his black prayer beads and fingered them, his head down, his mind counting the recitations.

I didn't know what to say, but I couldn't bear to have our meeting end like this, so I blurted out the first thing that came to mind. "It seems to me the Oriental perception of life is very different from the way we Westerners see it." I knew I sounded clumsy, and to cover my embarrassment, I quickly consumed the last of my orange juice and then pretended to be absorbed in watching a cluster of children playing at the edge of the Nile. The silence at our table stretched out like a desert as the waiter came and went, clearing our plates.

"You have no idea." Muhammad's voice had regained a teasing tone.

"Of what?"

"That word you just used, Oriental—"

"It was wrong, I know," I broke in. "An old habit. I didn't mean to be condescending."

But Muhammad shook his hand in mid-air to stop me and leaned forward across the table as though imparting a great secret. "Listen, that word has a special significance for us, which is different from yours. Oriental, in Arabic, means the original point of illumination. For us, the term Orient designates not so much a geographic location but a spiritual nexus. The Orient is the divine location from which the Light first became manifest. We also call it the place where the sun rises. As Suhrawardi taught, it is nothing less than the origin of all existence. You see?" He paused like a comedian waiting to give the punch line. "I told you that I would deliver to you the meaning of life!" He slapped the table lightly with the palm of one hand. As his tone became ever more buoyant, I had to bite my lip to stop from smiling, but the mischief in his eyes and voice was irresistible. "I like to think of myself as a fair and honest man," he said, spreading his palms wide. "But I am sorry to say, I am as racist as the next in my perception of who is of the Light and who is of the Dark."

I was taken aback. "You can't mean what I think you mean."

"Oh, yes, it is true," and now he put a hand over his heart in mock shame, all the while looking up at me from under a raised eyebrow. "I am racist because I associate the Occident with matter but consider the Orient as the original dwelling place of Light. Unfortunately, these ideas have become twisted in recent times, but in the early days, the years of al-Ghazzali and of Shihab al-din Yahya Suhrawardi, that great Shaykh al-Ishraq—" he said the names with such affection, and I envied him his teachers, though they were long dead "—in those days, our leaders were writing of the soul's yearning to free itself and return to its true home. And this, my friend, is a journey that travels from the West to the East, it goes beyond our differences with each other."

"Ahh, so then I should stay here if I want to get close to God, is that it?"

"You should certainly stay here." Muhammad looked at me so intently that my heart skipped a beat. "Or better yet, come to Damascus. There you will get closer still."

All I could do was laugh and make some flippant remark about time and money being no object. Muhammad kept his gaze on me for a second longer, then looked away and began again, "But your question deserves a serious reply. Physical matter can only be turned toward the Light by the luminous energy itself."

What in the world did he mean? I shook my head. But this time it was clear that Muhammad would not explain.

When we had finished our coffee and stood up from the table, the boy was suddenly at my side, looking up at me. "Good? Good?" he asked with exaggerated concern.

"*Quais*, good." I smiled, and glancing sideways I saw that Muhammad was smiling, too.

"Alhamdulillah!" the boy crowed as he darted back to prepare the boat for our return journey.

The sun, the good meal, and the intensity of my conversation with Muhammad left me feeling drowsy. I sprawled back against the cushions and watched larger river craft float by. I was about to doze off when Muhammad leaned in.

"Shall we continue with our lesson?" he asked quietly.

I looked up at him against the blue sky and nodded an assent.

"Ideas of the Light are not just something we intellectualize," he said in that same quiet voice. "They enter into all aspects of our life. Look over there at that mosque."

I followed the direction of his arm and hand, stretched across me toward the shore.

"What do you see?" he asked.

"A mosque," I answered, feeling foolish. "What am I looking for?"

"The Light is etched into the very stone of these monuments to God. Look there, first, at the minaret rising. See the crescent moon at the top? That is the subtle reflected light of Allah, as are the lights that will illuminate the minaret after the sun sets. Sometimes you'll even see the name of God written up there in neon. Yes, it's true," he overrode my half-voiced protest, "the electric light bulb has made it so very easy for us to express the wisdom we've always known." He lifted his shoulders with a shrug and said, "Well, why not?"

"Now look at the golden dome," he went on. "Some mosques have white domes, but this one is golden. We use gold and white often to assist the soul's memory of God."

"Like the Taj Mahal," I murmured, remembering one of the pictures in Bill's books.

"Yes. That beautiful lady." He looked down at me approvingly, then went on, pointing out the features of the mosque before it slid away. "Quickly now, look below, at the door. Do you notice the many small, carved cavities in the arch? These cavities are the niches for light that fills the core of every person's heart. The spark within us all, given by the greater Light, is physically embedded here." He tapped his chest.

"The light fills the core of our heart," I repeated. "But this is a metaphor?"

He shrugged again and smiled. "If you like. Or perhaps it is simply the truth."

We held each other's eyes for a moment, then he looked away. "The niche is duplicated inside each and every mosque, along the wall that faces the Ka'bah in Mecca. The *qiblah* wall, the wall with the niche," he said the words gently. "Some of our prayer rugs also have this niche for light woven into their design. You see the geometric emblems which decorate the building, yes?"

"They each have a circle in the middle," I responded.

"The center represents Allah, from Whom we all come forth. We have radiated out from that center, like rays from the sun, but truly we belong to the Source, and to that Source we will eventually return. In short, my friend," Muhammad summed up, "Islam is awash in the Light."

We kept our eyes on the shore, but Muhammad's presence and his teachings filled my mind. We stayed like that, silent, until we were jolted by the boat bumping up against the dock from which we'd departed hours before. Our young captain jumped out, offering us his slim hand as we, too, climbed ashore, and then stood at our elbows. His grin was as immense and eager as it had been that morning, but more anxious now. Muhammad reached into his pocket, pulled out a hundred pounds, an enormous sum, and handed it to the boy, but then he caught him lightly by the arm as the boy started to turn to me. "That's for both us," he said in English, gesturing between the two of us with his free hand. The boy grinned widely. No harm in trying, he seemed to be saying, before he scampered off in search of an evening's fare.

"Thank you," I said to Muhammad. "This day has meant more to me than you can ever know."

His direct stance held me. "We have not finished our conversation," he said. "You want to know more about Islam." It wasn't a question. "You must visit me in Damascus. Come, come this week."

"Muhammad, I can't just get up and go," I protested. "Arrangements have to be made. It's so hard to change tickets and itineraries and get the right visas here. And I leave for home in less than a week." But my voice trailed off under his steady gaze. Again the light danced in his eyes.

"Everything can be taken care of." He handed me a card with a phone number. He would be waiting at the Damascus airport when I arrived, he told me with complete assurance.

\*　\*　\*

Late that evening I slipped out of bed into the spill of light through the opening where the hotel curtains didn't quite meet. I moved a chair aside and stood quietly in the small cleared space. Then I raised one hand toward the ceiling, and pressed the other toward the ground, and slowly, slowly began to twirl. My white nightgown flared out as far as its narrow hem allowed as I spun faster and faster, my heart racing in the dark. Muhammad's voice eddied around me, until—

"Owwww!" I howled and let out a stream of groans. I'd whacked my shin on the bedside table, and now I collapsed back onto the bed, rubbing the sore spot vigorously. I had to laugh at myself, pretending to be a Sufi.

*You must have a guide.* Muhammad's voice was like a breath in my ear.

And that's when I knew I would go to Damascus.

As a child I received instruction
both in the Bible and in the Talmud.
I am a Jew, but I am enthralled
by the luminous figure of the Nazarene.

— Albert Einstein
"What Life Means to Einstein"
*The Saturday Evening Post*
October 26, 1929

# CHAPTER FIVE

# Christianity and the Essence of Enlightenment

A bright light will shine
to all parts of the earth
and many nations
shall come to you from afar.

—The Book of Tobit 13:11
*New American Bible*

The plans came together so quickly that I had to wonder what kinds of strings Muhammad had pulled and how he had acquired the power to pull them. There was so much I didn't know about this world into which I'd ventured, not to mention how much I didn't know about him. As I got on the plane, I had to admit that—for once in my life—I simply had to *trust*.

The flight attendants treated me like royalty, which made me wonder if Muhammad's influence extended even into the air. My fantasies flew ahead of me. I had only a few days for this adventure, but I imagined them filled with soulful talks, sightseeing, and (hopefully) instruction and possibly initiation into Sufi practice.

Always with Muhammad's melodious voice guiding me through every step.

"Oh, please, Jude," I scolded myself, "you're sounding spellbound." I turned back to my reading.

The plane landed with a series of stuttering bumps on the runway in Damascus. As I stood in the line moving slowly through customs, there was time for the flip side of my fantasies to play themselves out. What was I doing here? Why was I visiting this stranger on the spur of the moment? Getting out of Cairo at breakneck speed and planning to be back before my return flight to California seemed indeed fantastic. I'd given very little explanation when I phoned home to let John know I was going to Syria. And where was I going, where was I to stay? In Muhammad's home, I assumed, with Muhammad's family. He did have a family, didn't he? And I did want to stay with them. Didn't I?

Now I felt foolish. Was I a teenager creeping out of the house at night to meet up with a boy she hardly knew? Was I guru-struck? I decided to focus on my most immediate anxiety. Would he be waiting for me, as he'd promised?

Passing through the doors beyond customs, I was assaulted by the confusion of cries and shouts in languages I didn't understand from families and friends reuniting. And then, like an undercurrent, I began to hear my name spoken in a rich baritone. I spun this way and that, looking for the source of that baritone. Finally—there was Muhammad making his way through the crowd. Clasping me by the shoulders, he gave me that intent look and lightly kissed me on each cheek.

"Welcome," he said quietly. "Welcome. You have come."

Before I could catch my breath, he had picked up my suitcase, taken me by the arm, and was hurrying me toward his car. He walked with his head up, glancing neither right nor left. I must have had a funny sort of grin on my face, but he was too occupied with the logistics of getting us through the crowded and noisy airport to notice.

As we left the parking lot and barreled onto the freeway, I started babbling about the flight, about the graciousness of the attendants, about my enthusiasm for this unexpected trip.

Muhammad nodded his approval of everything I babbled, but he kept his attention focused on the driving. Finally calming down, I turned to the window and tried to take in the scenery, and suddenly another scrap of memory from my college religion class floated up. "On the road to Damascus," I murmured, then started wondering which road to Damascus Saul of Tarsus had taken into the city. Saul had traveled to Damascus determined to arrest members of a new sect, those followers of the teacher Jesus who would shortly begin to call themselves Christians. But a few miles outside the city, he had been struck by a vision and heard a heavenly voice demanding, "Why do you persecute me?" Blinded, he had holed up in a home in Damascus, neither eating nor drinking, until a Christian disciple named Ananias healed him on the Street Called Straight. On regaining his sight, Saul was baptized, took the name Paul, and began to preach, spreading the messages of Jesus and offering encouragement and instruction to the early Christian communities in present day Turkey.

Muhammad must have heard my murmuring, for now he spoke up. "They say Saul was a mystic," he said, "that he practiced an ancient form of Jewish mysticism called *merkabah*. Perhaps, then, it is no wonder that he too 'saw the Light.'" He did not take his eyes off the road, but I could see that he was smiling. "You see, Syria is not just an Islamic country," he went on. "There are many Christian sites here. However, since the days of Saul's conversion—yes, on this very road, yes, you have guessed it—well, my country has of course changed." He pointed his chin toward Damascus, almost as though he owned it.

Spread out before me was the "Green City." From this vantage point, Damascus did not appear ancient. Black ribbons of freeway led to a metropolis of high-rise apartments and towering office buildings. If I squinted my eyes, I could have been facing almost any city in the world. I started to ask about the area, but Muhammad held up a hand to stop me. "There will be time tomorrow for questions. Tonight, we celebrate." He glanced sideways at me. "I am glad you have come."

My stomach fluttered a little, but Muhammad seemed utterly calm as he navigated the busy streets without another word. An abrupt turn into the circular drive of a large downtown hotel gave me another jolt of surprise. "Muhammad…?"

"Our finest Western hotel," he interrupted. "You will be very comfortable here." Before I could say another word, he had leaped out of the car, spoken to the doorman in rapid Arabic, signaled a porter to take my bag from the trunk, and tipped them both.

"Muhammad?" I tried again.

He simply made a slight bow and ushered me into the lobby. Again speaking in Arabic, he gave my name to the check-in clerk and was handed a key.

We rode up in the elevator with the porter standing discreetly beside us. Now my stomach was turning flip-flops. What was I doing here, riding inexorably up toward a hotel room in a strange city with a man I didn't really know but with whom I was growing infatuated as my....my guru? Or was the proper word "guide"?

Muhammad opened the door to my room, but did not step in. "Take your time," he said. "When you are ready, I will be waiting for you in the restaurant downstairs. It, too, is one of our finest." In his tone I heard nothing but eagerness to please. He didn't seem guru-like anymore. And then he was gone.

Behind the closed door of my room, I began to laugh. "Okay," I told myself, "your imagination is clearly working overtime! He's gone off to pray, of course. Honestly, Jude, what were you thinking? You're overtired. Or maybe you're just hungry."

A bit teary-eyed, I reminded myself to call John as soon as I got back from dinner. And then I hurried to change my clothes.

\* \* \*

"You sound guru-struck," Rick was saying. I hadn't called John after all. I'd dialed Rick's number instead.

"But that's awful," I told him as I nervously fiddled with the dollar bill John and I had joked over. It suddenly seemed so long ago. "That can't be! I'm a rational human being! And this isn't the land," I cleared my throat, "of gurus!"

"Oh, please." He sounded like he was trying unsuccessfully to give me a reality check. "You're alone there. Your dream about finding the Light has made you vulnerable. You've met a fascinating, intellectual, mysterious man. You're a little swept away! Try to learn something."

"That's mean," I snapped back at my friend. "He's a Sufi, he's devout." I suddenly paused as reality hit me. "And I'm acting like a school girl chasing the math teacher! What have I gotten myself into?"

"Jude," I could hear him taking a deep breath, "breathe with me."

I huffed.

"Well," he said, and I could hear the smile in his voice, "I was thinking maybe a little bigger breath, maybe a little slower, but anyway, *breathe.*"

How could he find any of this funny?

"It's not that it's funny," he said, reading my mind again. "It's just that it's so understandable. There you are, far, far from home, and worn out, and it's all so new, and all these impressions are pouring in, all these new ideas… and there's someone to teach you things. It's perfectly normal. Happens with gurus all the time."

Was he laughing at me? "But this isn't like me," I protested. "I deplore people who chase gurus or who attach to anything!" That was the heart of it for me. "How could this have happened to me?"

He could hear that I'd begun to cry. "Okay, okay," he said. "No more jokes. I promise. Let's start over. Tell me from the top. What's happened so far since you've arrived in Damascus? Have you met his family? Gone to his ashram, I mean, mosque?"

"No. Well, not exactly." I cleared my throat, thinking and stalling for time as I tried to compose myself. "No talk of Islam," I said. "Or Sufism. Or the Light. This hasn't developed into anything like what I had expected. Just surface rhetoric. I haven't met any other initiates." That made me stop. "Rick, who am I kidding? This is ridiculous. And then when I pressed him to tell me more about the Light, he went on and on and at last told me he has a large and wonderful family. But I was still focused on my immediate here and now, so I asked him, 'Will I get to meet any of the other initiates?'"

"And?" Rick gently prompted.

"And he got this puzzled look on his face and said, 'There aren't any others.'" I let out a wounded yelp and buried my face in my free hand. "What was I thinking?"

Rick's voice stayed steady. "And then what happened?"

At last I took a deep breath. "Well, then…then…he… as soon as he heard my response, he looked bewildered… he looked sorry for the miscommunication between us. I'm sure he could see the frustration on my face. Then he pushed back his chair, stood up, made a low bow, and said something about our 'disconcerting dialogue'…and then he excused himself."

"You're kidding! Did he leave you with the check?"

"No, no, he took care of that." I took another deep breath to steady my voice. "But there I was, totally flummoxed and ashamed that I had followed this guy to—where? To Damascus, Syria, thinking I was going to study with a guy who I believed was, well…who did I think he was? God? So," I concluded, sounding even to myself like I was thirteen years old, "so I came up here and called you."

"And that was a good move," Rick assured me. "Now tell me this: do you feel safe there in that hotel? In your room?"

"I guess so." The thought hadn't occurred to me. "Yes. I do."

"All right, then. Now listen, Jude. I'll tell you this. The whole thing doesn't sound so terrible to me, at least not in the grand scheme of things. Though I can see how it would upset you," he hastened to add. "But it occurs to me to ask you this: is there anything to learn there? I mean, about the Light?"

And that, more than my bruised expectations, more than my disappointment, more than my unfamiliar surroundings, that was the question that kept me awake that night.

* * *

Early the next morning I was crossing the lobby on my way to breakfast, or at least to several strong cups of coffee before I decided what to do next, when a rumpled and bleary-eyed young man stepped in front of me tried to stop me with the briefest of bows. He spoke in broken English when I tried to push past him.

"Please, please," he managed, then held out a folded

slip of stationery with my name written in a wide fluid script across the outside.

I looked more closely at him and accepted the note, then moved to an area lit by a large lamp to read it. It was from Muhammad. *You have my deepest regrets for any inconvenience I have caused. Please accept, by way of apology, the services of my nephew Ziad as your tour guide for the day.* I glanced at the young man again, who now seemed to be dozing on his feet. Not much of a gift.

Muhammad's note went on. He proposed that I go to a village thirty miles north of Damascus, the town of Ma'aloula, one of only three villages in the world where Aramaic, the language of Jesus, was still spoken. I was to go to the church and ask for Father Luke. *With him you will be able to 'continue the conversation' in earnest. Respectfully yours, Muhammad.*

I walked to the front desk and asked the English-speaking clerk every question that came into my mind. Where was this Ma'aloula? How could I get back here, to this hotel, if I was stranded there? Had they heard of a Syrian Orthodox Church or of a Father Luke? The clerk had a reassuring response to every question.

Still unsure, I turned to Ziad and told him that we needed to have breakfast first. Then I strode into the dining room with Ziad moving slowly behind me and slipped into a chair before he even reached the table. I studied him and the situation as he looked everywhere but at me. Then he abruptly pulled an English phrase book out of his pocket. Flipping back and forth, he read something and asked, with the utmost seriousness, "Pardon me, Madame, but were peanuts offered your flight to Damascus?"

I couldn't help it. I began to laugh. And I found myself answering with equal seriousness, "Yes, yes, there were peanuts."

He smiled gratefully, whether at my reply or at his first big gulps of American coffee, I couldn't tell.

We stumbled into a fractured conversation, from which I gathered that Ziad had left school and was working part time for his uncle, to whom he was eternally grateful for his generosity and concern.

At these words, Muhammad's steady gaze flashed before my eyes, but I blinked it away. The boy's respect for his uncle was obviously sincere, and he was eager to drive me to the church in Ma'aloula if that was what his uncle—and I, he added courteously—wished.

I couldn't return to Cairo until at least the next day, anyway. What was I going to do with myself all day? Sit around and stew some more?

And so to Ma'aloula we went.

\*   \*   \*

The church towered above the whitewashed village. As we stopped in front of it, Ziad asked if he could wait in the car. He seemed so desperate for rest that I agreed. I walked alone up to a low doorway, turned the massive wooden handle, pushed open the heavy door, and stepped through. In an instant, all the traffic, all the commotion of Damascus and Cairo, all the trappings of modern life, all the topsy-turvy events of my trip were far behind me.

I was just beginning to examine the artwork and architecture in this old church when I heard a rustle behind me and turned to see a tall, thin man wearing a black robe emerge from some dim recess of the interior.

"I'm Father Luke," he said in remarkably good English. He held out his hand. "Welcome."

I introduced myself, and the priest nodded. "Yes. I was told to expect you." I winced. But his tone remained blandly cordial. "We do not get many American visitors here. You are most welcome," he repeated. "May I offer you some tea? Or something cool to drink, perhaps?"

He escorted me across a stone courtyard to the rectory next door, where we entered a cramped and musty whitewashed room littered with papers and church paraphernalia. This was obviously Father Luke's office. It was spartan and at the same time antique and mysterious. He took a seat behind a simple desk and motioned me to an old wooden chair. Through the tiny open window I heard the sound of a distant wind chime. I had no idea how to begin our conversation. After the emotional roller-coaster ride of the last few days, I felt drained and colorless. It hardly mattered that I was here.

A young boy appeared almost immediately with tea and biscuits, which he set on the desk. I was content to hold the glass that he poured for me and wait for Father Luke to begin.

"What brings you to Ma'aloula?" the priest inquired at last.

I gave him a hopeful look and shrugged my shoulders.

"I see," he replied. "Traveling is sometimes a mysterious experience." He paused. "For myself, in terms of geography, I have always stayed close to home." Clearly hoping to ease my awkwardness, he told me his own story. He had been born here in Ma'aloula, had taken his formal training in Damascus, and then had returned here. He had been with the parish for more than forty years and was now its priest.

"Life here is simple," he concluded. "And my parishioners' desires are simple. They ask only that I perform the sacraments and comfort them when needed." He seemed careful to neither inflate his own position nor that of the church itself.

I finally found my voice. "I'm surprised by your modesty. It doesn't fit my usual stereotype of the Catholic—or any—church. Perhaps this is what Christianity looks like closer to its roots?"

Father Luke took some time to consider what I had said. "This part of the world," he said at last, "is a mixture of the old and the new. Old cultures continually rub up against ancient religions. It is not difficult to be realistic about one's place under such circumstances." He paused again for a moment. "Dr. Najjar tells me you are interested in nontraditional viewpoints."

I couldn't help it. The mention of Muhammad's name caught me off guard. A sequence of images flashed through my mind—Muhammad in the felucca with the sun behind him, explaining Sufi symbolism for the Light. Muhammad last night, fumbling for words. What had he shared with the priest? I responded, "Then I'm sure he must have mentioned that I am interested in whatever hidden knowledge you may have about the Light of God. Would you know of such things?"

Father Luke studied me for a long moment, which made me fidget even more. "Dr. Najjar told me nothing specific," he said at last, "but I would be pleased to show you what some might call the 'hidden Christianity.' Come," he stood up. "Let's begin."

We walked back toward the church. The only sound was the whooshing of his robe over the time-worn cobblestones.

Inside the sanctuary, we approached the altar. In one corner, the small flames of white votives flickered against the gilded walls. Looking straight at me, Father Luke asked, "Have you ever wondered what the Second Coming of Christ will look like?"

I shook my head. *Oh, goodness,* I was thinking, *am I going to have to listen to an apocalyptic speech?*

"The Bible promises that when Christ returns, all nations will live in peace for a thousand years under one God. But as Christians are also aware, nearly three quarters of the world's population do not believe in Jesus as their savior. The Muslims hold to their understanding of Allah as recorded by God's messenger, Muhammad. The Hindus believe in Brahman as the Absolute at the core of the universe and have a pantheon of gods through which they access the divine. Buddha and his path to enlightenment are the answer for millions more; while Jews see it yet another way. How then is it that all nations will be gathered under one faith?" He paused. "But then, again, perhaps not one faith yet still under one God."

I looked up at him. These were not words I would have expected to hear from a priest. He seemed to sense my surprise because he shrugged as he went on, "People hold tightly to their preconceived notions of divinity and what divinity looks like and sounds like. The likelihood of all the world's religions turning instantly to Christianity or to any other faith is not plausible. But as Christians, we believe the Bible cannot be incorrect, either. So what will bond together every nation under one heaven, in peace, harmony, union, compassion, and acceptance of one another? What can all of the world religions simultaneously believe in?"

He turned and strode off down the aisle. I scampered to catch up. Suddenly I felt wide awake. We stopped under the Station of the Cross depicting Jesus falling under the weight of the cross. "The answer is clear," Father Luke said, "if you consider an alternative to human images. If the words of the New Testament are true, God will come out of the sky with an enormous demonstration of power." His voice began to swell. "What sign, what symbol would be so striking, so majestic, and so overwhelming that every nation would be converted at once in both heart and mind? The Bible says it is utter brilliance. Unyielding radiance. Pure Light!"

I felt as though he'd hit me in the chest. He went on, "Let me quote from the Book of Revelation, 'The city has no need of sun or moon to shine on it, for the glory of God is its light. The nations will walk by its light, and the kings of the earth will bring their glory into it. And there will be no night there.'"

After a pause, he looked straight into my eyes. "I do believe that this is the divine plan that will bring humanity together," he murmured. "Religion has been used for many purposes, often for the convenience of culture and politics. This cannot be divine, nor can it lead to salvation."

My eyes widened, "Does your church know about these beliefs, Father?" I hesitated. "How have you managed to escape notice so far?"

The corners of his mouth tipped up in a smile. "Ahh, we are a more complex institution than perhaps you realize. I am convinced, through study and prayer—and I am not alone—that the entire Bible is a great tribute and handbook to light, literally from the beginning of Genesis to the end of Revelation. Perhaps you know some of the verses where these references appear?"

I could only shake my head. Even on a good day, I knew very few Bible verses. And this was not a good day.

"'I am the light of the world,'" he began. "'I am the light, the life and the way,' and 'If thine eye be single thy whole body shall be full of light.'" He walked to the pulpit, on which a worn, massive Bible rested. Bending forward, he kissed the gilded cover in a solemn gesture of respect and reverence. A quiet air of sanctity pervaded the moment, and again I thought I heard the sound of a distant wind chime. Then, opening the book and nimbly thumbing through its parchment-thin pages, he read aloud example after example. "'The Lord is my light and my salvation.' 'Let us walk in the light of the Lord.' 'The Lord shall be unto thee an everlasting light.'"

This summoned forth another memory. "Father Luke, I think Catholics, in fact, hold that God is the absolute and pure light?"

"They most certainly do," he replied, then quoted a line from the Nicene Creed, "'God of God, light of light, true God of true God.'"

"But don't Christians say that the Light has to be Jesus?" I asked.

His reply was very careful. "That is a dilemma for this age, and it is the contention of some. But we will all one day realize that the spiritual teacher is merely a carrier of the greater Light into the world. Unfortunately, many believe that it is the *carrier* who is most important. Not the message. This clouds their vision."

"Wow."

That earned me a brief smile. "Let me show you a painting that may demonstrate the principle." He led me to an artist's spectacular vision of Paul's conversion. Paul's horse rearing, flaying the air, Paul's arm flung upward to protect him from the blinding radiance in the sky. Father Luke pointed to the short description posted below the painting: "'At midday along the road, your Excellency, I saw a light from heaven, brighter than the sun, shining around me and my companions' (Acts 26:13)."

All the research I had done after my dreams now began to tug at me like an insistent child. "I've never heard Paul's conversion called a near-death experience," I said, embarrassed to be speaking of NDEs with a priest, "but I see now that there are clear parallels between the two. Both speak of a primary brilliant light. Do you think it is possible, Father, that this is what really happened to Paul?" And suddenly I had such a dizzying sense of déjà vu that I swayed and would have fallen had the priest not grabbed my arm and led me carefully to one of the pews.

"I cannot adequately speak to you about near-death experiences," he began when it was clear I had recovered. "But the radical change in Paul's life clearly demonstrates the magnitude of his encounter. And his was not the only vision of God as an unearthly radiance that is recorded in the Bible. Ezekiel was a priest and a prophet to the peoples of Israel in exile. The book that bears his name in the Hebrew Scriptures recounts how the glory of God appeared to Ezekiel as a brilliant fire."

"Father," I ventured another heretical thought, "I have heard people say that the visions of people like Paul and Ezekiel were really sightings of UFOs...." But as my words tumbled out I could feel myself flushing with embarrassment to be asking this priest such a question. "Oh, heavens," I added, "do you think I've lived too long in California?"

Father Luke's expression remained serious, and now he sounded weary. I regretted putting him on the spot. "Those people, I believe, are trying to apply a material or physical interpretation to a mystical experience. Some people simply cannot understand that the spiritually devout have encounters with the Light." He closed his eyes for a moment, as though reconnecting with something almost forgotten. Opening his eyes again and watching me steadily, he continued: "I suppose the grandeur of their vision does seem above and beyond our world. But Ezekiel was promised that the burning vision of God he witnessed would one day be accessible to us all."

I caught my breath. For the first time, someone was speaking directly to my own experience. "As it was to Moses before him?" I offered, almost whispering.

The priest's eyes widened and then narrowed again. "Yes, indeed," he said and waited for me to go on. But when I could only glance away, he continued quietly, as though to reassure me, "My people's faith hinges on a Resurrection and its tandem partner, Ascension. The Shroud of Turin shows us that atomic light moment at Resurrection. And there are other examples, you know. The best known, of course, is the transfiguration of Jesus on a mountain in Galilee. That was when he revealed himself as a being of light to his three disciples."

Father Luke closed his eyes and recited, "'Jesus took with him Peter and James and his brother John and led them up a high mountain, by themselves. And he was transfigured before them, and his face shone like the sun, and his clothes became dazzling white.'"

The sun, the white, dazzling clothes—all references to the Light.

"Matthew 17, verses 1 and 2," Father Luke was saying. "The expression of divine radiance is everywhere. It is merely translated, if you will, so that we can access it here in this world."

"How do you mean?"

"Take the ritual use of light in the form of lanterns, fires, and candles in churches, altars, tombs, and holy shrines. We know that the candle itself isn't the Light, but we accept it as a symbol of the greater Light. Here, for instance, we celebrate with bonfires on our mountaintops in September. The whole valley is filled with the pious who have come to pay homage. It is a sacred and holy time for us in Ma'aloula. Everywhere there are fires and candlelight processions, and singing and chanting fill the night. One blaze after another is lit in prayer. It is a festival of light. We do these things based on an unconscious recognition of something greater."

I remembered what Bill had told me about the sun being absorbed into religious imagery. "Father, is sun worship mentioned anywhere in the Bible?" Now I felt I could ask him anything.

"Of course there are references to it." He paused, and then added in a whisper, "Many references." Walking back to the altar, he picked up a monstrance and raised it high in the air. He moved it from side to side as though he were showering the empty pews with lasers of light. He raised his face, still looking toward me, and thundered, "Behold the sun!" The monstrance, I saw now, was a circle of golden rays. My mind reeled. Akhenaten, Moses, Ezekiel, Jesus, Paul, the Light of the Sufis, and now the Light of Christianity. And the Light in my dreams. They were all connected!

"Accessible to us all," Father Luke repeated as if he were reading my thoughts. I looked up at him, and he, too, seemed radiant. And then he carefully set down the monstrance and turned back to me.

"Perhaps we should have more tea," he suggested. I had to laugh at this sudden return to the mundane, but he went on, unperturbed. "Or better yet, let me show you our garden and the holy spring which appeared miraculously for a Christian woman of Ma'aloula. Saint Thecla."

In the graying light, the whitewashed town lay half-shadowed on the slopes of the hill. In the distance, where the terrain flattened, a lone camel driver with his large herd moved across the desert. The air was peaceful and still. Father Luke filled a bottle with water from the spring and handed it to me. He smiled almost conspiratorially. "It has healed many pilgrims," he promised.

"There's something more worth mentioning." He pointed to the deepening sky and the single point of light that was the evening star. "Toward the end of Revelation, I think it is chapter 22, verse 16, Jesus says he is the bright morning star. Why do you think he says that?"

"Well," I fumbled, hoping to say the right thing, "the light of the star is easily understood."

"Yes, that's true," Father Luke acknowledged, "but Jesus is also identifying himself with the planet Venus. Venus, since ancient times, has been known as the planet of love. Jesus is telling us that he is Love and Light. His is a doctrine of love." He turned to look me straight in the face. "So often we become confused, transferring our vision of this perfect divine love onto one of our fragile and imperfect fellow humans. It is our great distraction."

He must have known, somehow! For surely with my guru infatuation, this is what I had done with Muhammad. I had mistaken the messenger for the message. I had certainly distracted myself from my own experience of the Light.

"It is not wrong to love," the priest added. "That is not what this means. Love is always a reflection of the Divine. But when we forget that we, like all spiritual teachers, are here to do just that—reflect the Light—then we become lost in a darkness of our own making."

I had the strangest impulse to kneel before him, but I recognized that that too would be mistaking the messenger for the message. "May I have...may I share in your blessing, Father?" I asked.

"You already do, you already do," he said as he

brushed his hand lightly over my forehead making the sign of the cross.

*     *     *

Ziad was sound asleep in the back seat when I returned to the car. At my approach, he awoke, alarmed at how late it had grown. Once on the highway, he sped back toward Damascus and struggled to pass along another message: "Instructed invitation, Madame, should you so desirous it, would please to come to villa for feasting this evening."

"What? Muhammad has invited me to his home?"

"Yes, Madame, precisely, precisely. Big feast, all family, much wished that you return with Ziad for evening. No problems for sleeping or airport tomorrow."

I was startled, but then I saw what Muhammad had done. He had asked Ziad to convey the invitation at the end of the day so that I would not be distracted or distressed during my visit to Ma'aloula.

"Yes, Ziad. It would be an honor to come." And I smiled at him.

"Good, good, very happy, all family come, you, good."

*     *     *

When we drove through the villa's gate, we were met by a crowd of about thirty people. Evidently, the entire extended family—grandparents, parents, aunts, uncles, and cousins—had gathered to greet me. I wondered what Muhammad could have said about me to create such expectations.

Then Muhammad stepped forward and, bowing low over my hand, helped me out of the car. "Thank you for coming," he said simply, but I could see an anxious question in his eyes. I smiled at him and nodded.

"You were right," I said quietly, "I have had an extraordinary day."

After that, private conversation became impossible as he introduced me to each family member, the crowd parting and then gathering behind us as we passed through. As we moved en masse toward the house, a few children darted in front to get a better look and then disappeared in the folds of the women's flowing skirts. I was clearly the center of attention. The courtyard was filled with color and the warm light of a Middle Eastern evening.

Muhammad's wife, Leila, who was taller than he, greeted me on the doorstep in a manner that was gracious and serene. Her kind look and warm welcome assured me that she had either not heard of Muhammad's and my "misunderstanding" or that she had easily accommodated it. Taking a deep breath, I walked into the house at her side.

The communal area was massive. Crystal chandeliers hung from high ceilings and beamed rainbows onto the walls, and below them, the inlaid tables of opalescent mother-of-pearl shimmered. Overstuffed couches bearing elaborate silver and gold-brocaded pillows ran along every wall. To my Western eyes, the decor was a kaleidoscope of colors and light. As we settled in the inner courtyard, which was cooled by a fountain and shaded by palms, I couldn't say enough to Leila and Muhammad about the beauty of their home. I began to let down my guard and engage in small talk.

Tea with fresh mint and plates of dates appeared. I let the flood of Arabic conversation wash over me. Maybe it was the safety of the home itself and the lively chatter that made me feel at ease. Whatever it was, I felt myself relax and let go more than I had during my entire journey so far. Fully enjoying the moment, I sipped the tea and looked around at Muhammad's family. At one point he caught my eye and smiled, gesturing, palms wide, at the crowd around him. And I understood. This was another offering, another gift to me.

Later, when we had moved inside, great platters of food began to appear. Appetizers of *hummus*, *kibbeh*, *samboosak*, pastry triangles filled with lamb and cheese, stuffed grape leaves—each dish more delicious than the last. Then came the main course, a *kabsa* of lamb stuffed with chicken, tomatoes, and onions. Fresh greens and lemons were arranged on the side.

As the talk subsided and the serious business of eating began, Muhammad turned to me. "Please, I would like very much to hear of your visit to Ma'aloula. Would you honor us with this story?" His tone was so sincere that I recognized immediately what he meant. Here was the true invitation to "continue our conversation."

And so I began to tell the family my story. Well, rather, though the room grew quiet and all eyes focused on me, I could see that some of them could not understand my English. I directed my story toward Muhammad, and he translated quietly for the others. But, mostly he plied me with questions, drawing out every detail of my discussion with the priest. I saw Leila following our conversation, glancing often at her husband. When I ventured at last to say, with the merest hint of a teasing tone, "Why, Muhammad, I had no idea you were so interested in Christianity," she laughed, her eyes twinkling at me above the hand with which she covered her mouth. And then, as Muhammad translated, the whole room rocked with laughter, repeating the joke over and over.

"I have much to learn," Muhammad said in a more serious tone when the laughter had died down. He looked over at his wife and smiled, then turned directly to me. "Sometimes my arrogance grows even larger than the sun. At such times, I am reminded of how far I have to go before I can even hope to be joined with the Light."

This time, with a certain pride, Leila translated for the family. As she did, I heard murmurs of "Alhamdulillah" all around me and caught the respectful looks and appreciative nods the others gave Muhammad in response to his admission.

I reported on my conversation with Father Luke, and then it was my turn to look directly at Muhammad as I offered the priest's closing remarks about love. "And then," I added, "surely some miracle must have occurred because the next thing I knew, I was asking for a blessing from a Catholic priest!"

And once again the room rocked with laughter as the translation made the rounds. Muhammad beamed back at me with a smile that spoke of a deeper understanding. "I am reminded of the words of the first president of Egypt, Mohammed Naguib," he said at last. "Let me paraphrase his words. 'Religion is a multicolored lantern. Everyone looks through a particular color, but the candle is always there.'"

"Alhamdullilah," I murmured, and I heard a chorus of approving echoes from around the room. Muhammad's statement struck me in a funny way. In that moment I realized I'd been looking through one or two of Muhammad's multicolored lenses. And now? What of the other pieces in the prism of many colors?

Soon the finger bowls filled with lemon water arrived and interrupted this private musing. Then, of course, came fragrant Arabic coffee spiced with cardamom. The servers lifted the coffeepots high above each cup and let a long stream of the strong liquid cascade into a target hardly larger than a thimble. Appreciative nods marked the appearance of foam at the top of each cup, indicating that the coffee had been brewed correctly. The ritual seemed to bind us into one tribe.

Toward midnight, Muhammad broke out the *hookah*, topped with burning charcoal on which apple-spiced tobacco was placed. A pipe on a long, flexible tube was passed from one person to another as we reclined on the sofas and pillows. I felt like a pasha, fed to bursting, surrounded by sweet aromas and the swirling colors and sounds of a large and boisterously loving family. Drowsy from the full day and the sleepless night before, I watched as a small whirlwind of light circled the room, alighting on each gleaming brown head of hair—

I dozed off and instantly jolted back awake. Had I been dreaming?

Muhammad, who was sitting beside me, noticed that I had startled. Yet he only nodded reassuringly, then swept his eyes once around the room and turned back to me.

"I feel like there's more to learn," I told him, "but I don't quite know what's missing or how to find it. Do you have any more wisdom you wish to bestow upon me?"

His eyes darted as he thought, "You know," he replied, "there are more pieces to the multicolored lantern. They are not found only here in Damascus. Perhaps you should travel onward and look for them. Perhaps...even as far as India." His voice trailed off.

I looked at him for a moment, puzzled again by the time travel leaps he so easily made. And then I smiled. This detour to Damascus had been nothing like my fantasies. But in the end, I had learned just what I most needed to learn. Perhaps Muhammad was my guide, after all.

Take up one idea.
Make that one idea your life
– think of it, dream of it,
live on that idea.
Let the brain, muscles, nerves
and every part of your body,
be full of that idea,
and just leave every other idea alone.
This is the way to success.

— Swami Vivekananda
*Vedanta Philosophy:*
*Lectures by the Swami*
*Vivekananda*
(*ca.* 1896)

# CHAPTER SIX

# India as a Salutation to the Sun

There is a light that shines beyond all things on earth,
beyond us all, beyond the heavens
beyond the highest, the very highest heavens.
This is the light that shines in your heart.

— *Chandogya Upanishad*

The next day Muhammad insisted that I use the phone in his private office to make whatever international calls I needed to rearrange my plans. I called my travel organizer, Gail.

When she heard that I now wanted to postpone my return home and travel to India, she immediately came back with "Ooh, I can just see you trekking in Nepal. With blinding white snow as a backdrop!" And she giggled just as she had during our meeting at the co-op. Then she sighed. "I'd better find you an open-ended round-the-world ticket so you can go wherever you need to go." And she did, at another miraculously low fare. As I showered my gratitude on her, she replied matter-of-factly, "Oh, stop. It's what I do. But I want to hear all about it when you get back!"

Still postponing my call home, I had an urge to call Gloria. Upbeat and peppy, she had been one of my closest friends since dragging me out of the dorm to go see the *Rocky Horror Picture Show*. A medical researcher by training, Gloria owned a successful lab in Berkeley. I was missing female companionship and especially her exuberance for almost everything.

"Girlfriend," I said when she answered the phone, "do I have a story for you," and I recounted the whole trip so far, including my guru infatuation—I was ready to call it that now—and its fortunate denouement. Gloria's exclamations of, "I don't believe it," and, "no way, get out," punctuated the tale. Her comments made me almost see her sitting on her bright pink futon in her living room.

When I finished, I heard her take a long breath, and then she said, "Well, it's clear I've got to get myself over there, I can't miss this part of your life. So, listen—" she kept talking right over the protests I had started to voice "—I've stockpiled weeks of vacation time and loads of dough. And the lab practically runs itself. So let's just say," I could hear her turning the pages of her organizer, "let's say I'll meet you in Delhi in eight days, and we'll go from there to…to…" I heard her pulling out the side table drawer where I knew she kept her maps of the world, largely to pinpoint the homes of her numerous international assistants. "Oh, well, of course," she said after a couple minutes of turning pages, "we'll go to Nepal, that's what we'll do!"

"Gloria, I don't know…," I began. "I set out to take this trip alone, and it seemed important at the time for me to travel alone…"

"Ahh."

A long silence on the end of the phone. Then I finally tried again. "I mean, if you really want to come...." Why was I feeling so apprehensive about including her in my plans?

"I do, Jude," she said. "But of course...I'm not going to intrude."

I winced. I couldn't admit that although I missed home and her, I wanted to keep this adventure all to myself. That I was afraid my experience would be less... less powerful with a friend from home at my side. Now I was feeling a twinge of regret that I'd called her.

"Gloria," I gave in, "I'll see you in eight days."

"Yes!" she cried, her enthusiasm exploding.

I had to smile. This was one of the reasons we'd been friends for so long.

And then, *finally*, it was time to call John. We'd spoken only twice since I'd been away, and that was shortly after my arrival in Cairo. Now the pleasure in his voice when he said hello brought tears to my eyes.

"How are you?" I asked.

"Good," he said, and I could tell that this was true. "Good," he repeated. "And missing you."

My heart squeezed tight. "I'm missing you, too," I said in a sheepish voice. I was suddenly feeling as though I'd betrayed him with the guru episode. To recover from that shred of guilt, I asked him to tell me about the little things. News of the neighborhood. How he'd spent the past weekend. What the yard looked like after the rain. His stories, all tinged with his idiosyncratic sense of humor, gradually allowed me to breathe easy again.

"So now you," he said. "How's the trip going?"

"Oh, John, I am learning so much!" But how could put all of it into these few words?

"You're getting what you wanted?"

I had to pause. "Yes. And I need to keep going," I added. A compulsion to go to India had been growing over the course of the night and the morning. It was as though it had always been my innermost desire.

"Go," he said, "Go. You've got to. It's all right."

And finally, at the sound of that familiar steady tone, all the emotion I had been carrying spilled over, and John held me, long distance, while I cried.

\* \* \*

With my arrival at the airport in Delhi, I realized I had left the West behind more completely than at any other point on the journey. The chaos that is India pressed in on me right away. The major offenses of the caste system had been outlawed, but evidence of its continued existence was everywhere. Palatial homes rose above fetid huts, richly dressed businessmen passed men in rags without seeing them. Dimly silhouetted behind the tinted windows of their black limousines, they rolled past barefoot beggars and cart drivers in filthy clothes.

Just hailing a taxi from the tangle of rushing humanity was an accomplishment that left me exhausted. From the taxi's window I saw crowds of Dalit, the "oppressed" or "untouchables," sprawled across the dusty paths that substituted for the sidewalks of western cities. They made the homeless people of California, in their cardboard-box shelters and filthy sleeping bags, look like paragons of order and cleanliness.

I thought about what Muhammad had told me about the distinction between the Occident and the Orient. But surely this could not be the "original point of illumination"! The Orient that was spread out before me seemed the very kingdom of darkness.

At first I'd objected when Gail had recommended I stay at the Maurya Sheraton, a Western hotel. "We don't want you laid low with any digestive distress," she'd said. At the time I'd protested that the fancy hotel would insulate me from a deeper experience of the country. Now, as I walked into the lobby with its clean appointments and familiar logo, starkly contrasting with my view of the streets from the taxi, I saw the wisdom in her plan and was grateful. Alone in my room, I drew the drapes and collapsed on the queen-sized bed. India was overwhelming. It was already clear that the Maurya Sheraton would give me a haven to retreat back to.

I had cut loose from my moorings in more ways than one, for here in India I had no plans or guides. Not even a guidebook. Gail's tour package had offered me some direction in Cairo, and Huda had led me further, and then Muhammad had steered me to Damascus and Ma'aloula. But in India? Here I hadn't a clue where to begin.

Later in the day, I wandered down to the hotel's gift shop, which was well stocked with English-language newspapers and magazines and a rack full of travel guides. Leafing through one, I came across a description of Varanasi, an hour's flight east of Delhi. Located on the banks of the Ganges River, it was, the book claimed, Hinduism's holiest city, a much-favored destination for pilgrims, and the place where Hindus hoped to die. I pictured another quiet, quaint village, rather like Ma'aloula, with some wise old Hindu sage, seated at the water's edge. He would lead me away from the squalor and darkness that cloaked this country and back into the light.

How naïve I was!

With the help of the Sheraton's efficient staff, my plans were made at Occidental speed, and I went to bed with renewed hope for my journey.

*   *   *

The minute hand jerked forward on the ancient brass clock in the small hotel where I was staying in Varanasi. The concierge had arranged for a guide and driver to pick me up at five o'clock on my first morning here, but it was already twenty-five minutes past. When I approached the desk, the concierge simply shrugged, looked up at the clock, and turned back to me with the fingers of one hand spread wide: "Five minutes. Please, madam, only five minutes more. Guide will come. Is very good guide."

I returned to the divan where I'd been sitting and flipped once more through the week-old copy of *Time* that I'd bought at the hotel in Delhi. But I no longer saw words, only a frustrated mental image of my wheels spinning in the sand.

Another ten minutes passed. I was about to go back to my room when a tall Indian man dressed in an immaculate white tunic, pants, and brocade slippers stepped through the hotel's high front entrance and crossed to the desk. I was on my feet before he had turned toward me.

"Good morning." His smile was broad, but his tone was maddeningly calm. "I am Rishi, your guide for the day. I am to show you Varanasi. I am told that you are curious about Hinduism." Yes, I had specifically asked for someone deeply familiar with the religion. "I have spent many years in study and practice at the Hindu temples and shrines," he assured me. "I will provide what information you wish."

"Your English is remarkable," I sputtered at last. My impatience at his being late had gotten to me. It wasn't what I'd intended to say. But his fluency did surprise me in this seemingly remote part of the galaxy.

"Yes," he said with a nod. "I speak several languages. As do most Indians."

I couldn't read his expression, but he had clenched his jaw at my remark. Again, my impatience prickled, whether at him or at myself I didn't pause to figure out. I simply uttered my own barely cloaked reproach. "Well, let's get going, shall we?"

The bow Rishi gave as he allowed me to pass by was several degrees stiffer than the one he had made in greeting me. "What would you like to see first?" he asked as he ushered me into the taxi he had hired for the day. He got into the front seat and turned to face me.

Again I felt overwhelmed. "But that's up to you!" I exclaimed. "I need to know about Hinduism."

"Ah," he answered imperturbably, and he turned away.

"Particularly," I plunged on, moving forward and

placing my hands on the back of the car seat, "I need to know how Hindus perceive God."

Rishi's head did not move for a long moment. When he turned, it was only to look out the side window of the cab. The silence seemed interminable.

"And what do you mean by 'God,' madam?" he asked at last, his tone neutral.

"Well, I...are you asking me to define God?" I fumbled.

That's when he startled me by turning abruptly to stare at me and smile. "Western ideas of God are so different from ours."

That slowed me down. "I think," I began, "that I am looking for something that goes beyond an *idea* of God."

He waited, his eyes never leaving my face.

"I am wondering...I mean, do you—do Hindus—ever experience God as, say, light? Are there beliefs in Hinduism that suggest light is divine? Are there sects that use light as a symbol for...you know? And would you, in particular, happen to know about that, about anything like...like that?" At last I got control of myself and stopped running on.

Rishi said something low and rapid to the driver, who turned right at the next corner. Then Rishi faced me again. "We will stop first at the holy Ganges River and the *ghats*." It sounded like a plan.

I went blank.

"The ghats," he repeated. "The steps and the funeral pyres where the dead are cremated. It is still early morning. Enough time to see everything, from beginning to end."

I pressed back against the taxi's sticky vinyl seat, vague images of funerals and fires rising sky-high running through my mind. A blare of the taxi's horn brought me back to the present, and I turned my attention to the world just beyond my window.

Varanasi was a maze of narrow streets and cramped alleys that all dead-ended in darkness. Hindu pilgrims and village residents shared the walkways with holy cows wearing ornate brass bells on their horns and around their necks. The clanging set up a counterpoint to the honking of horns as humans and animals stepped into the streets, oblivious of the oncoming traffic.

At the Ganges the scene was equally chaotic. Temples and palaces crowded the riverbank. I noticed stone tigers guarding the top of the house that kept the holy fire, while suns carved centuries ago stood at both ends of another roofline. Bill had taught me to read the language of symbols, but before I had a chance to ask Rishi about these images of light, he was leading me toward a stone bench at the summit of a small hill overlooking the river.

The *Insight* and *Lonely Planet Guide* books I read at the hotel were correct. "The sacred water was filled with daily life as men and women bathed, made offerings, or washed their clothing. It looked as if all humanity were taking part in this ritual, and it was impossible to tell if a person was good or evil, rich or poor, healthy or here to die. A sadhu shaved another and rinsed his blade in the murky river."[2] No wonder there was so much illness in this land, I thought. "Over the course of the day, blessed pilgrims gathered at Mother Ganga to wash away their sins.

---

2   See *Insight Guides India*, 9th ed. London.

Motionless holy men sat absorbed in rumination, their faces turned toward the sun in celebration of the endless cycle of mornings like this. The striking of wet clothing against the steps was accompanied by the distant ringing of temple bells, whose pitch and resonance varied with the preciousness of the material from which they were made—bronze, brass, or iron."[3] And over it all hung a fetid haze smelling of smoke and of—well, I didn't want to think what else.

I tried to turn away. I needed some small patch of clear space on which to rest my eyes from the over-whelming scene. But then Rishi stepped closer to me and pointed toward the funeral pyres. As I watched, the eldest male member of a family ignited the corpse. New flames leapt up where fires had burned low. The corpse was gradually consumed. As close as we were, the thick smoke, mingling with the morning mist, masked the sky and made it hard to breathe. I dug in my backpack for a handkerchief, a tissue—anything to cover my mouth and nose, to blot my stinging eyes. But I had no handkerchief. Soon I began to cough and couldn't stop. I was gasping for breath and taking in huge gulps of the sickening smell of (at least) burning flesh. I was afraid I would vomit.

Rishi leaned down toward me again. "You are uncomfortable, madam," he said with just a hint of sympathy. "Still, what do you see?"

"I don't know. It's too much. How can people—"

"Varanasi is the most holy city in India."

"This is holy? Crowds, filth, life, death. It just makes me want to run away." I fell into another coughing spell.

---

3   See *Lonely Planet: India,* 11th ed. Australia.

And he remained silent.

It was obviously a challenge. I forced myself to keep watching. A procession appeared, holding aloft a stretcher of fresh green bamboo on which was lashed a body wrapped in a shroud. The group proceeded and slowly, awkwardly, shifted the new body onto the pyre. The holy man's intoned prayers wafted up through the haze, and then someone took a torch and lit the new fire. After circling the body, friends and family stood silently by. Witnessing this intimate moment in their lives, I felt like a voyeur. Rishi remained motionless, and I made myself sit still, too.

It was an hour before Rishi spoke again. My nausea had passed. What I was feeling now was only an incredible weariness.

"Our religion teaches us how to break the cycle of *karma*." He turned to me. "Do you understand this term karma?"

"If I do something bad, something bad happens to me," I answered dully.

"Though it is true that karma refers to laws of cause and effect," he replied, "that our actions have consequences in the world, karma also refers to the progress of our souls toward God."

I looked up at him. His white tunic looked gray in the smoky light.

"Many people come here to the holy river, to Mother Ganga to die," he said. "Some arrive years before their deaths to prepare mentally for the last phase of this life-time. We believe that at death our soul rises up on the rays of the sun, but only those who possess the knowledge can break the cycle of their earthly lives and return to God permanently. Others must return to life here." He swept an arm out to take in the panorama of life around us.

It seemed clear to me why one would want to escape this life.

"They enter yet another cycle," he said, "in the pattern that you call reincarnation."

"But," I asked, "what knowledge is it that we must have in order to unite with God?" My wistfulness must have been plain.

Rishi's direct tone softened as he replied. "Our holy books contain the world's oldest religious records regarding the mystic Light. Hindus believe these books offer the knowledge necessary to break the bondage all humans encounter here on this earth. We must practice—there are different ways for different people—the adoration of God, the study of the scriptures, meditation, work. But the teachings are explicit. No matter the path, humans only receive true knowledge through contact with the mystic Light. In fact, the Light that shines in the highest world is the same light that shines within each of us. We are formed from it and we return to it."

"I have heard of other religions having nearly the same belief—" I started.

He interrupted me with scarcely concealed annoyance. "Please, we will speak only of Hinduism today!"

I wanted to describe the joy and gentleness of other religions and have him vicariously experience my cross-cultural interpretations. But Rishi's experiences and mine were clearly separated by an immense gulf. So I brought him back to what intrigued me most and what he was most comfortable with.

"And this contact with the Light," I said. "How do you get there?"

"As if it were so easy," he said a touch sarcastically, but also hopefully. But he smoothly continued. "Certain texts guide the initiate in how to reunite with the Light." And then he paraphrased as he recalled a passage from the *Mundaka Upanishad*:

> *The Knower of the Self knows the highest home of Brahman. There all is contained and shines brightly. The wise who worships without desiring happiness, transcends this seed, and they are not born again.*

He looked down. "The *Mundaka Upanishad* and the *Bhagavad-gita* are two of our holiest classics. The *Gita*," now he looked out at the Ganges, "speaks of a radiant river of light. Westerners…well, they often see a surface, and then they have no idea how to look beyond that surface." He gestured as if to indicate the whole city. "This is the City of Light. Is this not what you were looking for? I do not mean any disrespect, madam," he hurried on before I could react, "but if one cannot see the Light here, then one has not looked long enough."

I looked back at the scene around us; the chaos, the flashes of color and bursts of sound that still seemed overwhelming. But through the chaos I now sensed a rhythm, a pulse, like the heartbeat of humanity itself. Was this what Rishi meant by the City of Light?

"This is a place of death," he went on. "At death, we

all see the beautiful Light. This is the real significance of the name City of Light."

"Then there must be reports here of near-death experiences!" I cried. Maybe this would be my way in.

"We Hindus," he said in an expressionless tone, "do not have your Western passion to isolate God through science. We are content to accept that God exists."

I pressed on: "But how do you know you will see the mystic Light at death if you don't have near-death experiences to prove it?"

"Proof? Is not the word itself proof of Western disbelief?"

I was mesmerized by his question.

He went on. "Is the Western mind such that belief is only possible when an assertion can be validated by some application of logic or scientific 'evidence'? Is that the only path available by which the mind may arrive at truth?" He paused to breathe slowly and deeply, and then went on, choosing his words with care. "Doesn't the West find it onerous that religion has long been cognizant of things that you have only recently been able to discern, and then only with the dubious aid of science? We believe you will never achieve the knowledge this way! You need to break your bondage!" He sounded like a prophet. "If you do not believe, do not have faith, do not trust unflinchingly, you can never free yourself of the ties that bind you."

I took one last look at the vast tapestry spread out before me—the fires, the river, the washing, the priests, the palaces and temples, the sacred and the profane—and followed him back to the taxi. It was fascinating, hauntingly beautiful in its way. I could see that now, but how could anyone make the leap to see the Light itself in all this chaos, all this clutter?

As Rishi held the taxi's door open for me, he made another effort to help me understand. "You have heard of *tantric yoga?*" he asked.

Ahh, now this was something I knew about! "Yes," I said. "Mantras, mandalas, and female deities. There are rituals involved that I don't know, but during a mystical union between a man and a woman, who is supposed to embody the goddess, they can both reach nirvana." I spoke with a certain pride in my knowledge.

"Yes. We believe those are the ideas of a sensationalistic Western press that has misunderstood and distorted the sacred traditions of the East." And he shut the door with a snap for punctuation. Taking his seat in the front, he sat in thoughtful silence as the taxi crawled back into the heart of town.

Our second stop was a Hindu temple, where he resumed his lecture. "Tantric yoga is the path of integration. The West has misconstrued the true essence of tantric practice and ignored its metaphysical nature. It is true that in yoga an initiate can discover a sublime state of extinction from the physical body, arresting the breath, the semen, but contained within this extinction lays the absolute Light."

"What?" I was feeling like my head might explode.

He turned to face me, his eyes narrowed, but in his gaze I thought I saw the hint of a smile. "I will tell you a story," he began. "A disciple asked his guru, 'Sir, how can I find the true Light?' 'Come along,' said the guru, 'I will show you.' And down to the shallow lake they went, where the guru walked into the water and the disciple followed. And when they had reached the very middle of the lake, the guru suddenly pushed the disciple's head under the water. After a good long while, he released him, and the disciple came up gasping and sputtering. 'How did you feel?' asked the guru. 'I was dying for a breath of air!' the disciple replied. Then the guru said as he waded back to the lake's shore, 'When you desire God with the same intensity, you will find the true Light.'"

And with that, my guide opened my door and stood aside as I stepped out. And though we spent the rest of the afternoon visiting sacred sites and I was caught up in the swirl of color, scent, and life that seemed to fill the Hindu world to overflowing, Rishi said not another word about the Light.

\* \* \*

The water in the bathtub was a tad brown, but I slid in anyway and lowered myself below the surface. My eyes were squeezed shut, but I could feel my hair floating around my head and the air chilling my knees, which were jutting out like icebergs. I held my breath and waited.

Scenes from the day rose to the surface of my thoughts in rapid succession: The pungent funeral fires in the early morning light. The huge elephant, ablaze with painted designs, that had stood before me inside the first temple. His trunk thumped me twice on the head in blessing, then curled around my outstretched offering of paper rupees. The stele that had half-blocked the road. Dogs slept or peed on its base, monks circled it in meditation, bicyclists wove a cat's cradle around it. The chaos that was India seemed to pulse behind my eyeballs. Still I didn't come up for air.

I've always been a strong swimmer, so it seemed like forever before my lungs began to burn and press against my ribs and heart. I forced myself to blow out through my nose what little air remained, and fought the panic that began to creep toward me like a tiger in the dark. Behind my eyelids, sparks burst and spread, and when I opened my eyes, the same tiny explosions continued against a backdrop of black now, instead of red. My ears ached, my fingers and toes felt numb, and the nausea began to rise again as my mind's eye revisited the funeral scenes along the Ganges.

I burst back into the air, gasping and sputtering like the disciple in Rishi's story. Everything ached and burned—my head, my lungs, my heart, my arms and legs. I hung over the side of the tub, panting. I wasn't sure that I was any closer to the Light, but I knew that in the morning I would ask for Rishi again, and I would beg him—the word surprised me—yes, *beg* him to take me deeper into Varanasi.

Darkness cannot drive out Darkness;
Only Light can do that.
Hate cannot drive out Hate;
Only Love can do that.

—Martin Luther King Jr.

# CHAPTER SEVEN

# Buddhism in the Clear Light

Doubt everything.
Find your own light.

— Buddha
563–483 BCE

This time, the taxi turned straight into where one of the dark alleys dead ended and dropped us off near a dirt path leading up to a low, stone doorway. As we stepped into a tiny foyer, Rishi motioned for me to take off my shoes. I lined my plastic Chacos up beside a collection of woven sandals.

A low chanting wound its way toward us from the back of the house. Rishi scowled, muttered an imprecation, and then paused to take a deep breath as he motioned for me to hurry. I followed him down the narrow hallway, trying to imitate his posture: eyes cast down, left palm cradled in right hand and held just below the belly. I felt impatient. Why must we walk so slowly if we were already late?

The hallway opened into a large, bare room. Rishi

placed his palms together in front of his chest and bowed, and again I imitated him. Remembering how I'd told Rick about a dream in which I fell to my knees and worshipped the golden orb, I also suppressed a nervous laugh.

What would happen next?

Orange-robed monks, all of them with their hands in prayer position, each one standing in front of a low, round cushion, made a rectangle around the room. They were chanting a series of repetitive syllables—nonsense syllables, I would have called them. *Mo jo pro no.* They sounded like a child's song. Occasionally they bowed toward the front of the room where a golden statue of the Buddha sat on a raised platform. Surrounded by candles, the statue gave off flashes of light. It was shocking, this extravagantly glowing, golden statue in the middle of a world of poverty.

As the monks drifted down and sat on their cushions, Rishi led me to a pair of unoccupied cushions at the back of the room. Then he tried to demonstrate the correct posture, which was to sit on the front third of the cushion, the body's weight shifted forward to rest on the knees, shins, and feet on one's crossed legs. But when I squirmed, trying to get comfortable, he shot a stern look my way and shook his head once before resuming his own straight-backed pose.

Feeling defiant, I shifted again and was just spreading my long skirt across my knees to match the monks' neatly draped robes when, from somewhere along the wall to my right, a bell rang once, then again, resonating each time as the sound swirled around and upward through the room. Then everything became completely still. From

Rishi and the monks came not a sound, not a flicker of movement. I held my breath, trying not to shift or shudder, but soon my knees and back were stiff and aching from the tension of holding still. Then a dull throb began in my head and my nose felt clogged from the thin sweet smell of the incense that hung in the air.

I tried all the meditation techniques I knew, even reciting a mantra someone had taught me long ago in college. But my thoughts refused to be still. How long were we going to be sitting here? What was the point of just sitting? Why wasn't anyone doing or saying or chanting anything? Could I wiggle my foot, just this one foot that had fallen asleep, without being noticed?

I tried visualizing a rose and counted each petal as it opened in slow motion. But now I was becoming angry. Why was I here? Why was Rishi wasting my time? What was I going to get out of this sitting still? What difference would it make if I moved?

I started to roll my head to relieve a cramp, and instantly there was a sharp *clack!* from across the room, an ominous sound if I ever heard one, a sound that seemed to threaten punishment if I moved again. I felt caught, shamed, so now I sat there plotting an escape, then planning how I would tell the story of this spiritual "exercise" to John if I ever got out of here, longing suddenly for his compassion, his humor. My eyes stung, and I sniffed.

*Clack!*

Eventually, I grew incredibly weary, then bored. I counted from one to 10 under my breath, over and over, I chased daydreams around in my skull for minutes at a time. Soon I was forcing myself back to the counting. All I felt was a bitter combination of regret and self-criticism. I can't say how long this went on, but I would estimate at least half a day.

Finally, finally, the bell rang again, vibrating through my whole body this time. Rishi and the monks stood and bowed to the Buddha while I wobbled and nearly tipped over. Sharp needles of pain pricked up through the soles of my feet, I felt like my hips and knees had rusted into a half-crouching position.

Just as I managed to straighten up, the monks began a series of prostrations, bending like collapsible poles at the knees, hips, waist, laying their forearms and foreheads against the cool cement floor. I tried to follow, but I was not only stiff, but was also always a beat behind. Chanting poured over me, and then, just as abruptly, all sound and movement stopped. For a long moment, no one moved. I tried to catch my breath (quietly), but surely my neighbors on all sides could hear the thumping of my heart. At last the bell rang one more time, and the monks, Rishi, and I filed out of the room.

We collected our shoes and walked out again into the shaded alleyway. Still without a word Rishi quickly led me back out to the street and into the crowd. I hurried to keep up. We followed a maze of streets and pathways between leaning buildings until Rishi darted through another low doorway. I followed. We were in a café. He was greeted warmly by a woman in a bright sari who led us to a small table near the back.

"Rishi," I began impatiently as soon as we had sat down, but he raised one palm to stop me. Turning to our hostess, he engaged in a long, slow discussion in Hindi. It was the first time I would ever have called Rishi's mood congenial, and from the names of Indian delicacies that I recognized, they were clearly creating an elaborate menu for our meal. Only after she had walked away smiling did Rishi turn back to me and resume the stricter instructive tone I had come to expect from him.

"You have heard of the Four Noble Truths," he began, "and the Eightfold Path of Buddhist doctrine?" Assuming that I hadn't, he began to charge ahead into a lecture, but I broke in like an elementary school child eager to show that she had done her homework:

"Right Understanding, Right Intention, Right Speech, Right Action, Right Livelihood, Right Effort, Right Mindfulness, Right Concentration." I ticked them off on my fingers. "And the Four Noble Truths are about illusion—I mean, suffering—um," I was stumbling, "or is it both?"

My internal headmistress launched into her customary harangue: *You were assigned the proper books,* she said. Yes, back home I had picked up several classics on Buddhist thought over the years on my many trips to the bookstore. *If you had just read them thoroughly...*

I was saved when the waiter arrived with *lassis,* a heavily salted shake of creamy fresh yogurt with mint leaves on top. Rishi watched me, eyes narrowed, as I gulped mine down, hoping to cool my flushed face.

"The First Noble Truth," he said, "is suffering. The second is the cause of suffering, which is clinging." He seemed to stroke the word as he looked down into his own drink. Raising his eyes again to stare at me, he went on. "The third truth is the liberation from suffering, and the fourth is a way to live, a way to liberation, which is the Eightfold Path."

"By 'liberation' you mean enlightenment," I said. "Right?" I remembered the jeweled lights that had glittered and sparked off each ripple of the Nile during my felucca ride with Muhammad. Ishraq, the Arabic word for enlightenment, came back to me. I glanced around the dim café as though some stranger at another table might offer the insight I was needing.

Rishi, of course, was still frowning. "What do you know of the Buddha's enlightenment?" His voice was filled with challenge.

"He sat down under the bodhi tree," I sighed, certain that whatever I said, it wouldn't be what this guru was looking for, "and he meditated, and he meditated, and he meditated ...." I felt a flash of compassion for the lone figure sitting through the night. My knees still ached from the morning's session, and that had been less than a couple of hours.

Rishi was still speaking. "He raised his head and perceived the light of the morning star, and in that moment he experienced his awakening. The light of the morning star," he repeated as though I hadn't heard him.

My mouth must have been hanging open. "Jesus. Jesus says he is the morning star," I stuttered.

Rishi waved an impatient hand. "This was five centuries before Jesus!" And then some long-held resentment seemed to break loose in him, for he burst out, "Always, these comparisons, this 'ownership.' Always, this is the way of the West!"

"But that's not what I meant," I began.

But he regained his composure as quickly as he had lost it and picked up the thread of his earlier thought as though there had been no break.

"The Buddha's enlightenment was sudden at this first glimpse of the morning star. This is why the Buddha is often given the title 'Great Illuminator.' In this 'Clear Light' lies a freedom from suffering so pure that it feels like bliss. Very few achieve it. Very few." He shook his head and looked down again.

The waiter soon filled our table with heaped and steaming plates. A multihued vegetable curry whose flavors nearly spoke aloud in the aroma that surrounded us like a cloud. Bowls of white rice. A little tray laden with condiments—raisins, more yogurt, sliced fruits, and slivered nuts.

Rishi ate like one starving for many long minutes as I nibbled and watched him. When he spoke again, he began more softly. "Buddhists lead their initiates through innumerable light worlds. The signs along the way—fire, glowing insects, lightning, crystals, the sun—are all filled with light—*mystical light*, not physical lights." The condescending tone returned, even though I had not said a word. "'Do not let go of the sign of the Light.'" He recited Buddhist wisdom from memory. "'Which may be that of a lamp, or the glow of a fire, or the solar orb.'"

Shoving aside his empty plate, he snatched a pen from an inner pocket of his jacket and rapidly drew a design on the paper placemat. "A mandala," he explained. "You have seen them, perhaps most commonly in Tibetan art." This time he didn't wait for either confirmation or denial. "Look at it," he directed me in a cool voice.

I leaned forward so that I was looking straight down into the heart of the lopsided circle he had quickly drawn. Within its borders it held crudely drawn gods and goddesses like those we had seen in the Hindu temples the day before. I also recognized a lotus blossom, a series of triangles, and circles upon circles surrounding an inner square.

"Meditate on it." Another directive. Rishi pushed himself back from the table, stood up, and disappeared through a beaded curtain into the private reaches of the café.

I sat and stared at the mandala, but its chaotic design only seemed to reflect the jumble of sights, sounds, and experiences that had been pressing in on me ever since I had arrived in India. I pushed my hair back from my temples and stared harder, trying to force my mind to focus. The figures in the circle twisted and pranced like the flailing motions of my mind when I tried to still it. A long time passed. The restaurant had emptied before Rishi slid back into his seat. My head jerked up. He had caught me nodding off.

With one swift gesture, he snatched up the placemat, crumpled it, and tossed it aside. Before it could hit the floor I grabbed at it, caught it, and pressed it between my palms as I rushed to defend myself:

"But," I nearly shouted at him, "but you haven't explained what I'm looking for! How can you expect me to make sense of all this? You throw out little tidbits about the Light—but it doesn't add up! Do you even know?"

Rishi's dark eyes widened, and then he stood up and with great formality pushed his chair carefully under the table. "There is a taxi waiting outside to take you back to your hotel," he said in that neutral tone that had been driving me wild for two days. Then he handed me a folded slip of paper that I assumed to be the directions to give the driver.

I scrambled to pull his fee from my backpack, but when I held out the crumpled bills, a look almost of pity crossed his face. He placed his hands firmly behind his back.

"Do you think you can buy what you are looking for?" Those were his parting words.

In the taxi I unfolded the slip of paper. *The Buddha's last words to his disciples*, it read. *Be a lamp unto yourselves.* He had underlined the word *lamp*.

*     *     *

The smoky haze rising from the ghats along the Ganges stung my nostrils, just as it had on my first day in Varanasi, but now, on this last morning, I was able to sit with it, breathing in, breathing out, allowing the sights, sounds, and smells to wash over and through me with the rhythm of a wave. Then I noticed a prideful thought arising: *See how much I have learned in so short a time.* I managed to sidestep this obstacle by gently turning my thoughts to the people and events that had filled the last two-and-a -half days.

When the taxi had dropped me off at my hotel, I had gone straight to the concierge and explained that I wanted to find a Buddhist temple or school where I could take instruction. The concierge, an older man whose shape and attire reminded me of a very firm and very colorful beach ball, had responded with a stream of information:

"Ah, yes, madam," he began rather breathlessly, "you know, madam, Buddhism was born in India but very, very hard to find now so blended is it with Hinduism that you cannot tell where is the tail of one and the head of the other. I am a Hindu, madam, but there is much I love in the Buddhist way. And the venerable Dalai Lama makes his home in India, you know, madam." This sounded like high praise for His Holiness. Then, going on with his lips down turned and his palms spread wide in a gesture of regret, the concierge continued, "But you also know, madam, practicing Buddhists very, very hard to find in Varanasi, madam, only if you know the right people to ask, madam." His palms remained outstretched, eyes looking down.

When I pulled the rupees Rishi had refused out of my pocket, the concierge protested, but since he waved his hands toward the bills instead of folding them firmly behind his back as Rishi had, I figured it would be wise to insist that he accept them. Finally taking the rupees as though gathering feathers to his breast, he reached for paper and pen and jotted down the name and address of a small monastery on the other side of town.

"Please, madam, to say Rabindranath sends madam, and very, very kind Buddhist monks will care for madam, just as Rabindranath tells madam." He leaned into the name each time he pronounced it. Then he handed me the slip of paper with an overemphasized wink.

I spent two full days at the monastery, making the pilgrimage before dawn each morning and returning after dusk each evening. Rabindranath (or whatever the concierge's real name was) had been right. The monks were very kind, though none of them spoke a word of English. They taught me a few words of Pāli and Sanskrit and some chants from the Buddhist scriptures. For the most part, we passed both days in silence except when we were chanting, my own voice dropping to an unrecognizable depth as my breathing slowed. Long hours of sitting meditation were followed by excruciatingly slow walks through the temple halls and courtyard, each step achieved by placing the heel of the advancing foot beside the instep of the standing foot, inching forward in this way, eyes cast down and palms upraised and clasped at the belly. These hours were broken by meals consumed in stillness, except for the nodding and reaching and grunting and half-contained burping as we passed and savored the food.

Then there were my strange, mimed, one-on-one interviews with a series of monks, from rigidly attentive apprentices to their gently smiling masters, all of whom might be very young or very old or somewhere in between. I began to notice how my own body and mind responded to each monk. It was as though I could chart the electrical current ebbing and flowing as I connected with them. Together we stared at symbols—triangles, orbs, lotuses, the yin-yang (which reminded me of Rick's cats curled up together by the fire…it felt like a decade ago), even a swastika, which is an ancient holy symbol hijacked by an insane dictator. With the briefest and most intentional of gestures, the monks conveyed that each symbol held within it some combination of light and darkness.

I was making progress.

In my last interview, late on the second day, I pulled out the crumpled placemat on which Rishi had drawn the mandala. I saw the head monk's eyes light up as I smoothed it out in front of him. He bent over it for several minutes, perfectly still, his breath flowing so steadily that the whole room seemed to expand and contract with it. I matched my breath to his, as I had learned to do, and waited. When he looked up, he nodded to me, and I took my turn, imitating his posture of rapt attention to the rough circle and its circus of symbols rising on the crumpled paper. Again our breaths slowed, the room widened and narrowed around us, and my gaze gradually softened.

Nothing changed. Or everything did, for though monk, mandala, walls, cushions, and robes all seemed to remain the same, I felt at last—and only for an instant— the sense of peace that had eluded me since my dreams began.

I raised my eyes, looking for affirmation from the head monk, but he remained in the now-familiar posture of deep meditation, his eyes cast downward, his back straight yet soft, his breathing gentle and steady. For some reason, my usual impatience did not return. I seemed to watch myself settle into a matching pose, noticing—just noticing—that though the flood of peaceful feeling subsided, it left something in its wake. Or perhaps it was *the absence of something*. In any case, I could sit with it without the need to grasp at it.

I smiled at the thought. Rick had tried for years to explain the Buddhist concept of "not clinging," but it had never made sense to me. "But I want to cling," I used to wail. "I want the things I love." Now, without his help, maybe I was beginning to understand not the physical but the mental aspect of detachment.

Standing in a street above the Ganges, I turned my attention back to the chaotic scene that had overwhelmed me four days earlier. Slowly, as though back at the scene and taking infinitesimal half-steps, I focused on each object and every being, struggling, striving, bathing, chanting, and mourning along the river's banks. My gaze had just come full circle, back to the ghats and a renewed funeral pyre with a new procession making its way forward. I sensed someone standing stock-still beside me.

I looked up. It was Rishi. I let the laughter roll out of me. This was a fairy-tale ending to my strange stay in Varanasi.

But Rishi (of course) merely pressed his lips together, scowling as he had before and refusing to look back at me. So we stayed there for a moment, watching the scene together. Finally, knowing that time was running short if I hoped to reach Delhi in time to meet Gloria, I got up to go. But before I had gone two steps, a new thought stopped me in my tracks. I reached into my backpack and pulled out the mandala, unfolding it and smoothing it out once more.

Stepping back toward Rishi, I saw him glance down, sideways. With the briefest and most intentional of gestures, I indicated that the mandala and the scene spread before us were one and the same. His eyes flicked away, his lips pressed tighter still. I refolded the mandala, shaking my head, smiling a little, also grunting my exasperation.

I had turned again toward the waiting taxi when Rishi's voice stopped me.

"In Thailand," he began; his voice was huskier than usual, and he stopped to clear his throat. "In Thailand, I once visited a Buddhist temple. A golden structure, studded with jewels that ascended like pillars of fire toward the sun." He stopped as abruptly as he had begun. He had not looked at me, but now I could see the light glinting off the tears in his eyes, tears that brimmed but did not fall.

This time when I turned to go, something brimmed in me, too. Rishi's wall of impatience had melted, as had my own wall of stubbornness and judgment. The teacher and the student had become one, at least for a moment. I tucked the mandala away to keep it safe and reached for the taxi door, feeling lighter and happier than I had during the whole trip. I had not seen the Light, but perhaps there were other forms of spiritual success—or, better, spiritual progress—that could be just as sweet.

"Oh, Lord, forgive three sins that
are due to my human limitations.
Thou are everywhere but I worship thee here.
Thou are without form
but I worship thee in these forms.
Thou needest no praise,
yet I offer thee these prayers and salutations.
Lord, forgive three sins that
are due to my human limitations."

— M.M. Kaye
*The Far Pavilions*
(1978)

# CHAPTER EIGHT

# Honor the Light Within

There's too much darkness in the world.
Everywhere you turn
Someone is tryin' to tear someone down in some way;
Everywhere you go, there's a feeling of inadequacy,
or a feeling that you're not good enough.
I want to bring a certain light to the world.

— Alicia Keys
From a 2009 Interview

Two chairs cupped a small table on the verandah of the hotel at which Gloria and I had agreed to meet. Sprawled in one chair, I was slowly sipping a soda water with lime delivered by a soft-spoken, maroon-coated waiter. After my flight back from Varanasi, I had taken a long meditative walk in the garden, and now my mind felt smooth and deliberate as it swayed from thought to thought like the women I'd seen walking to the Ganges carrying earthenware pitchers on their heads. Breathing in, I caught the scent of an exuberantly flowering plant draped over the edge of the verandah. My imagination floated ahead to my reunion with Gloria. What would this long-time friend make of all the changes

I had experienced? How would I communicate the new spiritual power that seemed to purr inside me like a well-tuned motor just under the surface of the most mundane events, from dressing in the morning to, well, ordering a soda water with lime?

A small commotion at the curb in front of the hotel interrupted my musings, and, indeed, seemed summoned by them, for I heard Gloria's energetic voice rise above a stream of Hindi. "No, no, my good man," she was saying, and I watched as she shouldered a huge, overstuffed backpack and gathered up numerous smaller pieces of luggage from the motorized rickshaw from which she had just emerged.

I laughed out loud. Gloria could easily have taken a taxi from the airport, but the *tuk tuk* was so much more fun. Just like Gloria, I thought. "No, no!" she was saying now, "I will give you an enormous tip, but I will not pay twice the price you quoted when you picked me up! I mean, come on!" The haggling continued with gestures and raised voices until everyone on the verandah had gathered to watch the drama. I sighed, but I couldn't help noticing that both Gloria and the driver seemed to be enjoying themselves immensely.

"There!" she exclaimed triumphantly as she thrust a huge wad of rupees at him. "Good luck today," she sang out at him over her shoulder as she turned toward the hotel. And almost in the same breath, "Jude! Girlfriend! Isn't this *fantastic*?"

Gloria's arrival transformed the atmosphere. The formerly sleepy verandah had sprung into motion, and the oasis of quiet around my table was suddenly awash in luggage as Gloria dropped everything to sweep me into a full-bodied hug.

"Great!" she exclaimed, spotting my glass. "What are we drinking?" Her voice carried the length of the hotel's façade, and the waiter was instantly at our side, his serene demeanor now a lively animated one that matched Gloria's energy exactly. "Listen," she told me, "you must have something really, really delicious and very, very local." The waiter nodded and was away at once. "But not too sweet!" she called after him, and flung herself into the chair opposite mine. "Girlfriend, it's so good to see you! Tell me everything! I am so glad to be here, I can hardly stand it; I feel like I've been let out of my cage!" And she rattled on, throwing out questions and interrupting herself before I even had a chance to open my mouth.

My carefully constructed equilibrium vanished. I felt the old familiar squeezing in my chest, a sensation I thought I had left far behind.

Taking a deep breath, I tried to calm my jumpy mind. In a moment, as Gloria's chatter flowed on and gathered me in, I began to recognize in her the manic vacation energy of the newly arrived. I knew she would settle down. Under more ordinary circumstances, she was the best of listeners. There would be time later to share my story.

Gloria's enthusiasm was unabated the next day as she swept us off on a whirlwind tour of Delhi. It was a monstrous undertaking. All my initial overwhelm—at the chaos, the crowds, the poverty and abundance jostling cheek by jowl—returned in full force. We traipsed

through temples and bazaars, Gloria chatting and haggling with tour guides, merchants, even beggars on the
street. My increasing exhaustion flared into irritation.
I was jealous of her ability to take this chaotic country
in stride. My own hard-won insight and acceptance had
disappeared under the daily assault of sights and sounds.
I couldn't seem to find my footing. Or catch my breath.

It was my breathlessness that finally caught Gloria's
attention and brought her race through the city to an
abrupt halt. I was leaning against a fly-bedecked fruit
stand, quietly gasping for air, when she was suddenly at
my side.

"Jude, hon, what is it?" she said in a volume pitched
for intimacy for the first time since her arrival.

"I'm all righ—" I tried to wave her off.

"No, you certainly are not all right," she said firmly.
"We're finding a quiet place to sit you down right now."

This was easier said than done, of course, but Gloria's
determination, focused now on her new mission, found
us a taxi, then an isolated corner in our hotel's restaurant.
As soon as the steaming glasses of aromatic tea had been
placed before us and our dinner orders whisked off to the
kitchen, Gloria began again.

"Now, Jude, what's wrong? How long have you been
feeling this way?"

"Nothing's wrong." I stopped. How to describe what
I was feeling? I took the path of least resistance. She was a
medical researcher; so I started with the symptoms. "I've
been having this tightness in my chest."

"Tightness?" She practically pounced on the word.
"Jude, you're having chest pains, shortness of breath? We

need to get you to a doctor." And she stood up, rattling the table and splashing tea onto the tablecloth.

"Gloria." I mustered all the firmness I had left. "Sit down. Please."

Looking doubtful, she lowered herself back into her chair.

"It's not a heart attack." I was speaking more clearly now. "You don't have to call the medics. I promise. It's just ..." I spread my fingers wide. "It's hard to explain, but every time I run up against some obstacle...or I stray... or something happens on this, this path I'm on, my chest squeezes shut and I feel trapped and breathless. It started way back in California."

"Uh-huh." She had switched gears at last, but I still felt wary.

"I thought...in Varanasi that I'd found what I was looking for. Or something close to it. But now it's gone again." My eyes stung, and I felt childish and pathetic.

"Tell me about Varanasi, Jude."

The moment I'd been waiting for had arrived, but now I was stymied. "I— I can't. Nothing happened. And everything did." I didn't know where to look. "Well, that sounds stupid."

"No—no, it doesn't. Listen, hon, I think you're tired, too tired to go out tonight. Let's save all this till tomorrow when we're both rested."

"Yes," I whispered. "If I could just have some time... spend the morning alone, get back to my practice."

"Whatever you need."

But I felt a renewed twinge of impatience. She hadn't asked about my practice. Wasn't she curious at all?

*   *   *

Although I spent hours in meditation the next morning, trying to regain the calm, centered focus I'd achieved in the monastery in Varanasi, it was hopeless. My thoughts chattered and scurried and one wave after another of anger and impatience rose up like a wall. When I got up from my bed pillows, which I'd folded over to make a cushion on the floor, I felt even more frustrated than I had the day before. Later, waiting for lunch, I couldn't repress a dark scowl as I saw Gloria bustling toward me. Her face, in contrast to mine, was positively glittering with excitement.

"Well, girlfriend, I've found the solution to all our problems!" As usual she began before she'd even sat down. "While you were doing your thing—" she waved her hands in the air to cover whatever it was that I'd been doing "—I got busy, and I found us the most fantastic palm reader! No, listen," she stopped me before I could protest. "Listen. You know the best ones in the world are right here in India. So I went to the front desk first thing this morning and asked for a recommendation on the best of the best, and, Jude," her voice dropped an octave, "Jude, you will not believe how amazing this woman is! I've made an appointment for you."

"Oh, please, Gloria," I was finally able to interrupt her. "What are you thinking? I haven't been interested in that kind of thing for years. No put-down intended, but you know, I've grown out of it."

She sat still for a minute, completely silent, studying me. "All right. Can I just tell you what happened to me?"

I nodded, and she launched into a detailed account of the reading she'd received. Evidently this woman had recounted Gloria's whole work history and had capped it off by describing her current experiments and offering suggestions about what she should explore next.

I had to laugh. "Gloria, you mean to tell me an Indian palm reader is giving you advice on cutting-edge Western medicine? And you're thinking of taking it?"

Gloria's own laugh came galloping out to join mine. "I am! It sounds crazy, but I'm telling you, Jude, this woman was amazing. I wish you'd go. I think you should just see for yourself."

"See for yourself," Rishi had told me. "See for yourself," the Varanasi monks had communicated over and over during my two days with them. Besides, I couldn't bear to break the closeness that Gloria and I had started to recapture. Fits of giggles were still ricocheting back and forth between us.

"Oh, all right." I gave an elaborate sigh of resignation, and we both laughed again. "All right," I said. "What time did you set me up for?"

*     *     *

Having threaded our way through a maze of alleys in one of the poorer parts of Old Delhi, we found ourselves standing in front of a heavy teakwood door punctuated by polished brass hinges and heavy door knocker. The elegance surprised me in this neighborhood. Gloria was practically dancing with excitement as she pounded the heavy knocker against its brass plate. A tall, turbaned man, whom I guessed to be in his twenties, opened the door almost instantly and ushered us in. His grandmother, Madame Samsara, a name he pronounced without a hint of irony, was expecting me.

"Well," Gloria said, "you won't be needing me." She promised to return in about an hour.

Smoothly and with an air of charm, the young man led me into a cool, dimly lit parlor and gestured toward a seat on one of the low divans that lined the walls. Curling trails of incense filled the room with an acrid scent, and all around me stood intricately carved figures of gods and goddesses, both fearsome and merry. The young man, promising it would be "only a moment," disappeared down the hall.

But the moments stretched out, and my head was beginning to feel heavy when I was roused by the sound of a querulous older voice erupting in Hindi to protest something the young man was saying. Then an ancient woman appeared in the doorway. Their heated discussion ceased abruptly as he took her hand in a firm grip. I suspected she was his great-grandmother, if, indeed, she was any relation at all.

"Good afternoon," I said, rising and picking up my pack. "This must be an inconvenient time—"

"No," she croaked. "Please you sit here." She pointed with one claw-like finger to the chair on one side of the tiny table in the center of the room and fixed her huge, unblinking eyes on me as I took my place. Madame Samsara had broken free of the young man by now, and she tottered with remarkable speed to a large armchair drawn up to the other side of the table. The young man was watching her anxiously, but she only gave him a brief nod as she pulled a small lamp closer to us by its cord. He disappeared and she held out her hands to grasp mine.

Madame Samsara examined my left palm, then my right, then my left again. Next, she extracted a pencil and a small pad from an invisible fold in her multi-layered silk sari. She scrawled a number of indecipherable marks on the pad, then began to draw a hand, her pencil wobbling, the line squiggling with her effort. Her breath bathed my palm with a fine mist. She bent my fingers back and forth, pinching the pads at the base of each finger and squeezing the folds between them. From time to time she pressed a fingertip on a line in my palm as though to hold her place while she tried to reproduce it in her sketch.

For the second time that day I tried to meditate, breathing in and out roughly in rhythm with Madame Samsara. But the discomfort of having my hands pulled and pinched and prodded distracted me. I was just about to pull away when she flung down both my hand and her pencil and sat back in the huge chair. Her dark almond eyes, rimmed in thick black kohl, blinked at me like an owl's.

"You are thirty-nine years old."

"Forty."

"No!" she cried, and then, as she scrambled forward again, she grabbed my hand and began the painful process of drawing my hand all over again. "You have lost a year," she said accusingly.

"I don't think so," I said. "But it's all right," I hurried to reassure her, realizing I couldn't wait another century for her to draw my hand again. "Can you tell me anything else?"

She remained silent, her head bent doggedly to her task. With a huge sigh, I relaxed and let her do what she needed to do. At least I was inside, where it was quiet and somewhat cool.

She spoke again. "You are an excavator." Her voice held the same certainty as before.

"Noooooo," I drew the word out skeptically, but she interrupted.

"No, no, no, not an excavator like those who dig in the dust. But you are excavating…here." She rubbed her hand over her chest.

My own heart skipped a beat. "Maybe so," I murmured.

"I will tell you the story. Two, three months ago, you wake up," she declared.

Was she referring to my dreams of the Light?

Before I could ask, she plunged on, describing my talks with Rick and John, my visits to Bill's subterranean lair and the guru-itis that had led me to Syria and the side trip to Ma'aloula. "How do you do this?" I asked. It was, as Gloria had said, amazing.

In the middle of a word, she snapped her mouth shut and began staring at me. I shifted in my chair. Why should this old woman's gaze make me so uncomfortable? Suddenly I felt a burning in my chest, a sweeping sensation like a hot night wind, rising and as quickly subsiding, leaving a space in me that felt clean and dry.

"How," she said. It was not a question. "Yes, you, I will tell." Gone was the flat and scratchy voice, the voice of the crone, with which she had recounted my story. Now, as she told me her story, her voice grew silky and musical.

Palm reading had been a family profession for a very long time. It was something she learned from her father in a faraway village. She had passed it on to her children, and then to her grandchildren. "But India is changing," she said. "It is more free. My grandson will not continue. He does not approve." A mischievous smile flickered across her face, then was gone. Ah, so that was the text of the argument I had overheard.

Behind her, shafts of light streamed through the slats in the wooden lattice on the window, turning the specks of dust in the air into tiny glittering jewels.

"But how do you do it?" I asked again, more a murmur than a demand.

"You saw." She gestured to her drawings. "Sitting silent, I draw the palm. It is a very slow process. I know." This time she smiled broadly. "I am tuning myself to the lines, so to contact the record of this person." She nodded toward me. "When the lines become clear, all I do is read." She shrugged her shoulders as if it were simple. Then she added an afterthought: "From the *Akashic Record*."

I sat forward in my chair. "Can you explain that?"

"Everything belonging to each soul—actions, words, thoughts, deeds—are written on time and space. This is the realm we call the astral light, or Akasha. The ether that spreads throughout the universe. The practice requires much training. But when one learns to align with the higher will, then it is possible to contact the Akasha. Actually," she added, her voice growing softer, "records from all time are available. They are easily viewed if you approach them properly."

She closed her eyes and leaned her head against the

high back of her chair. She continued at a murmur so low I had to lean across the table to hear. "One day during meditation, before my career was beginning, a vision came. A beam of light pierced through my body, here to here." A gnarled hand drew a line in the air from her forehead down to her navel. "Beautiful, it was beautiful," she whispered, "like a million diamonds. From then on I knew I would be able to read the Akasha."

Without moving her head, she opened her eyes and fixed me again with a slowly blinking gaze. "You have had such dreams, dreams still vivid even now. Dreams of the Light."

And then…a subtle incandescence seemed to flow up from the carpet and out from the couches and pillows all around us, as though their colors were melting and spreading through the air.

"Yes," I breathed, "those dreams are precious to me." And the tide of longing that the dreams had left behind rose like a sob in my throat.

"A glimpse of the divine can come through the dream state," she said. "There are Tibetan Buddhist monks who have made this into an art. They called it dream yoga. Every night the initiate must stay conscious as they fall asleep. Eventually one encounters the Dawning of the Clear Light. This happened to you. I do not know why, for you were not prepared."

Madame Samsara swiveled her head as though to catch a glimpse of the rainbow gems that danced over her shoulder. Startling me with a sudden western inflection in her voice, she returned to her train of thought: "But they drive you now, these dreams. They are your mission."

"Perhaps they brought me here?"

She did not move. Again she struck me as a wise old owl.

"So," I said, taking a deep breath, "tell me more about this dream yoga."

"It is no longer exclusively the practice of Buddhist monks. There are masters now in the West who call it by another name." She cocked an eyebrow at me.

I shook my head. "I give up."

"*Lucid dreaming!*" she crowed triumphantly.

"How do you know so much about the West?" I had to ask.

Instantly her smile was gone. "The Internet," she intoned, and then she leaned forward and put her elbows on the table. We were practically nose to nose so that when she shook a finger in my face, I had to blink.

"The ecstasy of uniting with the beautiful orb does not happen all the time. Only with high moral development, special intent, and humility. With Rishi—"

The mention of his name made me sit upright.

"—with Rishi," she went on, sounding like she was giving me grandmotherly advice, "you were two souls on the same quest. All you were missing was…"

"Humility." I said it with her and cringed.

"We draw to us the teacher we need," she said in a kinder voice. "Each one mirrors where we are on the journey and helps us move along…move along." She scooted her hands through the air as though shooing something along. Then she held her palms up facing me, as if to say, "Stop." She added, "Your next teacher is already at your side."

I was about to ask if she was by any chance referring to herself when the door opened and her turbaned grandson entered, carrying two glasses of iced tea and a crystal pitcher of liquid sugar on a shimmering silver platter. As he poured a thin stream of the clear elixir into each glass, he kept his eyes on Madame Samsara. "More, more," she croaked, giving a fine imitation of senility. I hid my smile behind my own glass and turned to take in the rest of the room. The light was dimming, but the rich colors still glowed. At last my eyes lit on a small framed painting whose title clearly read *Om Sweet Om*. I nearly sprayed out a mouthful of tea.

"What's that?" I pointed.

"Ah," Madame Samsara interrupted her negotiations with her grandson. He quickly left the room. "Ah, you have found it." She seemed delighted. Reaching for my arm, she struggled up and nearly dragged me across the carpet. "Look, the middle area is radiant energy. It says, *Om*. This is the Eternal Word of God. When God created the Light, a sound occurred simultaneously: *Ommmm*," she repeated. Even in her reedy voice, the sound hummed and swelled around us.

"This is the Big Bang theory captured in a religious picture," she went on. "The moment of creation produced not only light but sound. Every language is rooted in this sound we call the eternal word. You see? Light streams out from the center, and at the end of every ray, there is a name. In this picture you can see the names of all the dialects in my country. That is the real message of this picture. You know," she patted my hand lightly, "there should be a book written about the Eternal Sound, as well." Her eyes were twinkling. She waited for me to figure it out.

"Help me out," I begged.

"The radiant orb loves variety," she said. "That is why the earth has so much variation. The rays represent variation, but we must never lose sight that everything, ev-er-y-thing, comes from a single source." Changing tempo, she added, "Like the yogis, we can train our midbrains to connect with the eternal sound and light.[4] From now on, you must view them as partners."

"'In the beginning was the Word, and the Word was with God, and the Word was God,'" I recited. "That's a parallel, isn't it, in the Gospel of John!" I seemed to be learning to hear the connections that Bill had taught me to see.

But Madame Samsara had already turned away, and I thought for a moment she hadn't heard me. She was tottering back to the table under her own steam, her arms slightly outstretched for balance. Yet as she caught hold of the back of her chair and began to lower herself into it, I heard her sing out softly, "There is always a parallel, always, on the way to the Light."

\* \* \*

By now the room was deep in shadow. For what seemed like hours, we had been engaged in a kind of game, free associating about the Light. Madame Samsara spoke

---

4    See Dr. Pillai's Midbrain Miracle Method for specific techniques, *mmm* meditation, and how sound creates intelligence. http://www.pillaicenter. com/midbrain.aspx

about the Star of Bethlehem, I remembered stories about sightings of the Virgin Mary that had been preceded by a flash of Light. When she mentioned Edgar Cayce and Shirley MacLaine, I smiled, but by this time I was no longer surprised by her knowledge of Western culture. She also spoke of prayer groups that sat in a circle, passing the Light from member to member, compounding the spiritual energy for the recipient of their prayers. And somewhat shyly, remembering Rishi's harsh reactions, I mentioned my very first associations with the Light and my research into near-death experiences.

"Not just near-death," she corrected me, "but death itself." She leaned her head back and closed her eyes. "In India the vultures are always circling. In the villages we encounter death daily. We sit with our dying as they journey onward." She flipped a hand through the air as though souls could vault into heaven like circus per-formers. Then her eyes became slits so she could watch me. Her words made me think of the work of Elisabeth Kübler-Ross. "Before they leave us, they tell us they see lighted figures coming for them; sometimes they are given white clothing to wear. I have seen the dying become like lights, their faces glow radiant, and their eyes..." Her eyes closed again. "When it finally comes, death need not be unhappy."[5]

Silence. For a long time Madame Samsara did not move. I began to feel uneasy. Had she worn herself out? Had she fallen asleep? Should I call her grandson?

I was reaching a tentative hand toward her when she

---

5   See *On Death and Dying* by Elisabeth Kübler-Ross (New York: Touchstone, 1969).

suddenly sighed and roused herself, shaking her torso slightly like a bird settling its feathers. Her wide eyes looked calmly at me. "Meeting with the Light, uniting with the Light, is the preeminent spiritual fulfillment," she said. "But it is not the meeting that results in dramatic change. The Light creates euphoria; you feel sooooo goooood." She drew out the words, and I nodded back. I remembered that feeling. "It is a feeling of the most profound love. And it is this love that leads to the permanent alteration. It can happen in a dream, though this is somewhat rare. It is what all those in religious devotion long for. Union with the love."

She paused, then went on: "Life is really a practice ground for love. At death, when you encounter the Clear Light, you know like that—" she clapped her palms together "—how well you have loved while you were alive. The more you love, the easier it will be to unite with the beautiful orb when you die. If you do not practice or live much love, then, at death, as you come face to face with your soul, you will not like what you see. It is really very simple." Now she began putting her pencil and pad away in the same invisible fold from which they had come. "Very, very simple. 'God is love' means God *feels like* love. We all discover that in the end." Suddenly she stopped and looked straight at me. "Spiritual anthropologist," she said in quite a different tone.

"What?"

"You. You are a—"

But in the middle of the sentence, the door flew open and there was Gloria, beaming.

"Well? Didn't I tell you?"

Again Gloria had burst in, breaking the mood. I looked across to catch Madame Samsara's eye and share a shrug, but I found the old woman transformed. Her face was softened and suffused with light.

"You! Here again!" she exclaimed as she hauled herself to her feet and lifted her puckered face to be kissed.

"Oh, you wonderful woman! What have you been telling my friend for all these hours?" Gloria had taken the old woman in her arms and was towering over her.

Madame Samsara's eyes, peering out from under Gloria's embrace, swiveled round to mine. "Ah, you know…"

And then, I could swear, she winked at me.

When there's light shining on a tree,
that tree takes on a different meaning.
If there's no light at all it just looks dead.
If you look at light as godly meaning,
the world comes alive in a certain way

— Matisyahu
Reggae and Alternative
Rock Musician

# CHAPTER NINE

# Science in Another Light

Science without religion is lame,
religion without science is blind.

—Albert Einstein

A pair of eyes, brightly painted on the gleaming white walls of a Buddhist temple, glared out at the maze of prayer flags looped across the temple grounds. I stood baffled at the sheer number, each a heartfelt message sent upward to any gods that might read them. The Tibetans believe that when blown by the wind, the prayers stamped on the flags spread goodwill and compassion. They also feel that harmony is achieved when the five elements— sky, wind, fire, water, and earth—are balanced.

"Ah!" Gloria exclaimed, as she had a hundred times since we'd left Kathmandu two days before. "Look, Jude!" she pointed at the zigzagging yards of rope from which fluttered flags in blue, white, red, green, and yellow. "A spider web to catch the gods!"

I squinted up at the scraps of cloth. "Good luck," I said dryly. The web looked decidedly empty to me. "This must not be on their flight plan."

171

"Ha!" She turned to our guides, pointing and gesturing, weaving a spider's web with her fingers, flapping her arms and tracing a pattern in the sky, her attempt to share the joke. The three men, two Sherpas and a Newar from Kathmandu, nodded and smiled; the shortest of them even threw back his head and laughed as he had when he'd first met Gloria in Kathmandu.

"You are funny," he said.

"No, no," Gloria protested, "my friend…" and, grinning, she pointed at me.

He bowed in my direction. "You are funny," he repeated.

I managed a smile and a nod in return.

I hadn't been talking much ever since we'd left Madame Samsara's, and Gloria had, for the most part, been leaving me alone. She was in better shape than I was and must have guessed that I needed to concentrate on the path just to keep up.

I had gotten it into my head that at the top of the mountain I would encounter the Light again. For this reason alone, I kept doggedly striding forward. Madame Samsara had said I needed "high moral development, special intent and humility." Right now I was focusing on "special intent." The Himalayas promised to take care of humility.

I had gotten my first humbling view of the mountains as our plane had flown north toward Nepal and I saw how the early morning sun struck sparks off the mammoth blanket of snow that stretched to both horizons and half-way down the slopes. The glare had been painful to my eyes, and seeing the ragged peaks of Annapurna South and Machhapuchchhre[6] had made me feel dizzy. And, I asked myself, are we going to walk into that snow? Gail's words echoed in my ears: *I'm getting another vision of you! Now you're trekking in Nepal, with blinding white snow as a backdrop.* I felt tired just thinking about it.

Dealing with the details of preparing for the hike—finding a good agent, making sure their equipment was top notch and that their Sherpas were highly experienced—had been a relief during our days in Kathmandu. Here at least was something I knew how to do. And the first day and a half of hiking had been easier than I had expected. Still, even though my daypack was lighter than the others, my shoulders were already aching. The trail wound on dirt paths through lowland villages and past well tended fields and Buddhist temples of every size and shape. At each turn and crest we came to, villagers stopped, placed their palms together, and bowed and said, "*Namaste.*" Roughly, a salutation meaning "the spirit in me bows or acknowledges the spiritual element within you."

Now, as we left behind the temple with the kohl-rimmed eyes and the web of prayer flags, our path began to climb and the air grew chillier. Gloria strode along with her head held high, her eyes and nostrils flaring as though she didn't want to miss a single sight or scent. But the guides were looking closely at the ground, walking carefully over the stones and around the small boulders that littered the trail.

Suddenly Rajendra Man, the gentleman who had found Gloria so funny, swooped down and plucked up

---

6    A holy mountain that has never been allowed to be climbed.

a softball-sized rock. Hefting it in his hands, he spoke excitedly to his companions, Ang Pemba and Tenzing, who came close to him. Using a smaller stone, Rajendra Man chipped away at his rock, and then, while his fellow guides chattered encouragement and advice, he selected one of the boulders and hurled the rock against it. It cracked precisely in half. Rajendra Man was grinning broadly. He showed the inside of the rock to his friends but carefully shielded it from Gloria and me. Then he folded the rock back together and with a flourish presented it to Gloria.

"Ah!" she exclaimed again when she pulled the two halves apart. They all laughed this time. Inside was the fossilized print of an unrecognizable creature. Rajendra Man, Ang Pemba, and Tenzing spoke all at once in a mixture of English, Sherpa, and Nepali. Their exaggerated gestures seemed to be miming an ancient story.

Gloria tried to interpret. "I think they're saying these mountains once lay under the sea. And this is a stone from God, created millions of years ago when the island of India crashed into Asia, pushing the land up to what we now call the Himalayas. They think it's very auspicious that we should find this stone as we begin our ascent. Here, Jude, look!"

I held the two halves of the rock in my palms and stared at the glossy black mass inside. The creature's skeleton was clearly outlined. I handed the treasure back to her. She tucked it in her pack and mimed our thanks to the Sherpas and Rajendra Man.

Then we set off again, climbing steadily now.

*   *   *

Dusk. The last light was melting, creating a more diffuse but somehow more powerful light in the not-quite-darkness. A magnificent vista spread out before us. Fireflies had begun to dance, and the night, as it deepened, seemed to burst with pinpoints of light.

Sitting on the grassy slope outside the teahouse where we were camped, I grabbed at a firefly, missed, and grabbed again. The insect bobbed away, appearing and disappearing as it turned its miniature light bulb on and off.

Squatting beside me, Gloria said quietly, "Trying to hold on to a bit of Light?"

She startled me. Suddenly I saw that this was exactly what I was doing...and had been doing throughout my trip. Or even before, ever since my dreams had begun. I took a deep breath and let it out in a laugh. "It's not working, is it?" I said. Finally, in the dusk, it was becoming clear that I could no more hold the Light than my clumsiness could catch a firefly.

Now I turned to my friend. "Gloria, you're a scientist..."

"Ye-es," she grinned as if to say, "Duh!" and then waited for the question.

"Can you explain this to me? How do these creatures make light?"

"Ah!" She caught herself repeating her favorite outcry and glanced at me. I rolled my eyes, and for the first time that day we laughed together. "Well," she began, "some creatures have the power of self-illumination, and the fireflies are one of them. Plankton and some kinds of fish are others. It isn't actually electricity, you see, but chemical activity that looks like light. We call it bioluminescence."

"Bioluminescence," I echoed, watching the fireflies blinking on and off.

"They make me think about the miracle of electricity," she went on. We were staring across a black lake at a Nepalese village nestled into the foothills. The houses were lit only by the fires burning within. "I mean, it's only been a little more than a century since the world—some parts of it, anyway—first had access to electric light. One hundred measly little years in all the vast expanse of time," she continued, her voice hushed now. "For all of recorded history, people have been without the light bulb, virtually in the dark when night fell. And now we've lit the globe. Our lights are so overwhelming that astronomers complain they can no longer see the stars."

"Except here," I whispered back, pointing at the dazzling night sky. "On the Rooftop of the World." Our travel brochures had trumpeted the phrase. Now, sitting on this steep hill high in the Himalayas, with the stars blinking just beyond the fireflies, I could believe that this was exactly where we were: on the rooftop of the world. So close I could almost touch...

"The Light," I said slowly. "We're surrounded by symbols of it! Medicine's healing with lasers. Electric light, and photography, and movies, and computers—they're all related, aren't they? And everywhere I've gone...Akhenaten, Moses, the Muslims' niche for light, the Christians' tradition of God as light and love. Then the Buddhists and the Hindus, Madame Samsara with all those miracles she talked about. And now—bugs!" I grabbed at another firefly and laughed when I missed again. "Could the technological dawn emerging on the planet correspond to a spiritual dawn occurring inside us? You know, kind of inner meets outer? I know I'm rambling, but do you get my point?"

Gloria was looking at me thoughtfully. "Hey, you know what you are?" I shook my head. "You're a spiritual anthropologist, that's what you are. I think you've found your calling, girl."

"Gloria—did Samsara tell you that? Or did you tell her?"

"What? What did she say?"

"Those very words. 'Spiritual anthropologist.' Whatever that means."

Gloria flung one long arm around me and hugged me to her sideways. "You'll find out," she promised. "Maybe it's written on one of the sacred Mani stones that line the mountain trails."

"Or because it's so difficult to attain, perhaps at the top of the mountain?"

"Maybe. Come on, Light-Catcher," she gave me a hearty pat and stood up, brushing off the seat of her pants. "If we're gonna climb tomorrow, we'd better get some sleep tonight."

\*   \*   \*

It was midmorning when we arrived at another tidy village. My head was pounding. I hadn't slept well at all. Between Gloria's snoring and the rattling of my own thoughts, I had lain awake most of the night, finally getting up in frustration when the Sherpas stirred at dawn to build our breakfast fire. At least the huge tree in the middle of this new village promised a place where I could stop and rest.

But as I leaned my head back against the trunk, I realized that the whole village seemed to be filing past me, and every man, woman, and child had a chicken or small pig slung under one arm. The crowd was shuffling toward a rope bridge suspended over a shallow riverbed. Above the opposite bank rose the walls of an open-air temple. Holy men were sitting near the bridge. Tenzing murmured that they lived off the alms they begged from the crowds on days of sacrifice like this one. One of these *sadhus*, a huge man with wild eyes and a straggling beard, sat motionless on a nearby hill, staring over the heads of the passing villagers. I guessed that he was meditating and was chagrined to see Gloria sneak closer to take his picture. He didn't move.

Rajendra Man battled his way back through the crowd. "Come," he said, "I will find a most excellent spot. You will see everything." We scrambled behind him, foregoing the bridge and wading through the shallow waters. The icy stream made my feet and ankles ache, so that now I hurt all over. I was beginning to wonder if I was coming down with something. Gloria squealed and high-stepped across as fast as she could. At the top of another hill, we turned and, looking where Rajendra Man pointed, we saw the whole temple yard spread out below us. It was covered in bright red blood. My stomach lurched.

"It is the day of Kali," Rajendra Man announced.

Once a week, he explained, the villagers made a sacrifice to this goddess of death. The animals were being slaughtered wholesale, their freshly-cut arteries squirting over a statue of Kali so that the goddess dripped with blood, as did the temple walls. The stone floors ran with rivulets of the thick red offering. The assistants' robes were splattered in gruesome patterns. The vinegary smell was so sharp that I could taste it in my mouth. The murmur of chanted prayers rose over the scene. It was the same chant I had heard in Varanasi with Rishi. Now it pounded in my temples as though trying to get out.

I stumbled down the far side of the hill, hoping I wasn't going to be sick. The others eventually joined me, but when they looked at my pale face with concern, I waved them off. "Let's get going," was all I said.

During our stop for lunch, I sat shivering on the ground some distance away from Gloria and the Nepalese crew. Though clouds wheeled overhead, the snow on the slopes above and around us was still blinding. Ever the gentleman, Rajendra Man brought me a plate of freshly caught fried fish, but the smell made me turn from him, gagging. He stayed crouched beside me for a moment. When I didn't turn back, he returned to the fire.

Nevertheless, when the others had finished their lunch, I was the first to stumble forward. I was overcome with exhaustion, and I wasn't sure why the morning's ritual had left me cold and shaking. All I knew was that, more than ever, I needed to get to the top.

\*    \*    \*

"Excavating. You are excavating here." Madame Samsara's face came close as she dipped her crippled fingers toward my breastbone and began to pull my rib cage apart—

I woke up coughing. My chest hurt where she had touched me in my dream. But it was Gloria's face that leaned close, her features blurred by the tears in my eyes.

"How are you, hon?"

"D-dream," I gasped.

"I know." She put one cool hand on top of my hot fist and slowly eased my fingers flat. "Fever dreams. We make the wildest connections." She stroked my forehead, gently pushing back the damp hair. And I dozed off again, caught in fever.

\*    \*    \*

"Hey, stranger, you're awake!" It was Gloria again, and it occurred to me that I must have been asleep for a long time. I was suddenly thirsty. As though she could read my mind, Gloria offered me some water. Just as suddenly, I was eager to hear what she was saying. How much had I missed already?

"Go on," I gestured weakly through the pounding headache.

"Well, the whole deal works on light," she said. "See, all of life runs on what are called circadian rhythms. That's rhythms that are determined by the periods of light and dark in each twenty-four hours. From the lowliest insect to the highest mammal, all creatures are regulated by these rhythms. Take hibernation and bird migration. Both behaviors are triggered by the quantity of light available in a day. Or look at how bees tell the rest of the hive where nectar is located. They use a dance that describes the angle of the food from the sun."

Her voice, like her face, swam in and out of focus. Still, I wanted to participate in the conversation. "Egypt," I whispered.

"What, hon?" She leaned in closer.

"Ancient Egyptians…a thought came…bee was…a sun insect." I got it out. Then I shook my head. "More," I mouthed and added a smile. "Please?"

"Well, okay." She plunged on. "Isn't that kind of amazing about the bees? I mean, isn't it amazing that my knowledge of science gets backed up by your discoveries in religion and culture? Together, I swear, we add up to a whole brain!"

I tried to giggle with her but ended up coughing till I was breathless.

"Whoa, girl." She supported my head while I took a sip of water. "That's it, not another joke for the rest of the day." She waited until my breathing had grown steady before continuing. "Instead, we'll talk about sheep. Nothing funny in sheep. Just that we've found that fertilization and conception times for sheep are regulated by the amount of light during certain times of the year. "And get this—" the excitement crept back into her voice "—we humans may be sensitive to light just like sheep!"

"Get out," I murmured.

She laughed. "Yep. You can set your biological clock on that one! But it's all about humility, really…. I think we human beings try to set ourselves apart, refusing to acknowledge that since we, too, are part of the animal kingdom, we just might have many of the same sensitivities as other creatures. In the last few decades, we scientists have begun to appreciate the effects light has on us humans. For instance," she reached out to brush a lock of hair back from my temple, "there's a gland in our brains that's sensitive to light. You've heard of the pineal gland, right? Well, it turns out it's photosensitive. See? We now believe that out of all the light that enters through the eyes, only a small bit gets used for vision. The rest of the light affects this master gland in particular. And there are even people who profess that gazing at the sun during safe times will heal the body through regulating the pineal gland and perhaps the pituitary gland as well.

"And here's something we're gonna be thinking about a lot in a few days," she finished. "Each of us may be able to control the amount of jet lag we get from our flights home by monitoring the amount of light we receive before, during, and after the trip."

The thought of going home brought a wave of simultaneous disappointment and desire so strong that I had to turn my head toward the tent wall. Gloria kept on stroking my hair, and her words dissolved into a tuneless hum as I felt sleep overcome me again.

\* \* \*

Madame Samsara ladled a steaming spoonful of light and brought it shakily toward me. "Vrroom! Here comes the airplane," she said. "Open wide..."

For two more days I hovered in and out of feverish consciousness while the others waited.

*   *   *

"Jude! Fantastic, you're awake!"

I could measure my recovery by the amount of energy Gloria allowed herself to express.

"Look what I've found! I bought this little metaphysical book when we were in Kathmandu and I've finally found the time to read it, and I've been learning about chakras—which I guess are like vortexes of energy that reside in different parts of our body—and all of a sudden I come to this picture of a guy, a mystic-type guy, with light streaming in and out of his head. 'The opening of the crown chakra.' Doesn't that sound delicious? But here's the kicker, Jude: this light has got to be flowing through the pineal and pituitary glands."

I raised my head to look at the picture and thought of Madame Samsara's "Om Sweet Om" with the rays of light pouring out in all directions.

"But what's even wilder is DMT." Gloria was really excited now.

"What's that?"

"Oh," she said, "don't worry about the long scientific name[7] right now. It's enough to say that it's a chemical made mostly in the pineal gland and is being called 'the spirit molecule.' That little chemical is the

7   DMT, N,N-Dimethyltryptamine, is a psychedelic compound of the tryptamine family. Called the "spirit molecule," it is naturally produced in the brain by the pineal gland and is thought to give rise to paranormal experiences.

doorway to other realms of consciousness, near-death experiences, and the like. It's the physical proof we've been looking for that connects us all worldwide. And it's been suggested there might be a specific region, literally a 'God part' of the brain that's DNA-wired into us."

I looked up at her glowing face and felt my smile grow to match hers as she spoke of these marvelous connections.

"I just remembered something else," she said. "Some scientists speculate we'll someday use nanoparticles of gold to fix our DNA when it goes awry. They're saying our DNA is really a double-helix wire of light and that the future of medicine resides in repairing our light-bodies through our DNA.

"Wow," she added after a minute, "this is what you've been getting at, isn't it? Deep down, we know that the physical and the metaphysical are linked, that science and religion aren't opponents, after all, but partners. All this scientific stuff is validating ancient held religious beliefs... well...isn't it amazing?"

I pondered her words, then said, "I think it's a piece of the puzzle I've been looking for. And you know what else is amazing?" She shook her head. "I think I'm hungry."

\* \* \*

Tenzing still had me on a diet of spicy soup, which he brewed from ingredients that Rajendra Man and Ang Pemba collected at the Kali village, as I called it, the place where we had witnessed the ritual sacrifices. I didn't want to know what those ingredients were. I was just grateful to be sitting up and holding my own spoon.

I had been sick with a fever for three days, but on this evening, I felt washed clean, as cool and dry as I had been under Madame Samsara's gaze. Gloria and I had been sitting for a long time just outside the tent, wrapped in our blankets and watching the fading light.

"Is it time for the fireflies yet?" I asked at last to get her started.

"Maybe not." And then she grinned. "But we've got our own internal firefly action going on, you know."

I raised my eyebrows to encourage her to go on.

"Well! Biologists have found that the human body is a virtual sea of electricity and light. We've got chemically dependent synapse activity going on in here every second." She tapped her chest, her arms, her thighs, her head. "And those messages leaping across the synapses are just like the intermittent light that fireflies give off. They're like tiny sparks that transmit chemical instructions throughout our whole body, which means that our nervous systems actually respond to and understand light frequencies."

"But here is what I really love!" she plunged on. "Using an electron microscope, we can watch the process of fertilization in humans. And get this. At the very moment when the egg and sperm unite, we see this chemical reaction that looks like an explosion of light! It's like those tiny cells are imitating the first moment of creation!"

We both held our breath. "Say," I started slowly, "didn't I read a while back that some scientist discovered the light of creation? He claimed to 'seeing' ancient light, traveling from so far away in the universe that it must be from the beginning of time. There have been some lively responses to that 'discovery.' It caused a big flap, I guess, but anyway…he compared it to looking directly at God. I wonder if he—"

"Oh, he saw the Light, girlfriend; you bet!" Gloria finished for me, and we both laughed.

"You know what's really cool?" Gloria started up again, her own synapses firing. "Photosynthesis," she said, relishing the word. "Because in plants we can best see how light actually produces physical matter. Maybe that's why living foods are energetically better for health because they resonate with us. There are chemical reactions akin to light in our food, especially live foods. Live foods help us shine physically, and the resultant health lets our souls shine through. That's the connection between food and spirit." She giggled at her ability to so aptly tie up the whole foods movement in a sentence or two.

At this I lifted my arms out from under my blanket and extended them straight toward the earth, my fingers spread wide.

It was Gloria's turn to cock an eyebrow at me. "What are you doing?" she asked in mock surprise.

"I'm thinking of that Akhenaten symbol in Egypt," I explained. "The one with the little hands extending from the sun. See, if the disk—the Light—is equivalent to energy, then the rays are like a bridge or maybe a path, which is the process of creation itself, the link between the creator and the created…and so then the tiny hands represent physical matter. So Akhenaten got it, didn't he, that light creates matter. *At the highest level we are light bodies.* Or possibly, it's Einstein's theory in a religious symbol!" I rotated my hands like weather vanes, sending imaginary rays of light over all our surroundings. Gloria jumped in, waving her arms like windmills and singing the theme song from *Star Trek*.

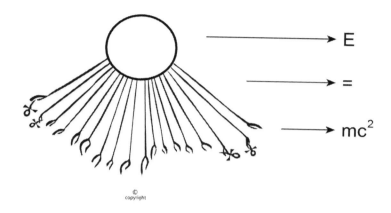

E

=

$mc^2$

© copyright

In the midst of our goofiness, something small and joyful began to percolate inside me, rising up from someplace deep and tender, someplace that was healing. Could Gloria's enthusiasm be contagious?

"You are funny!" Rajendra Man was suddenly by our side. We dropped our arms and cleared our throats, but all three of us couldn't help laughing.

"Excuse me for disturbing your dance," he said, wiping his eyes. "But I must tell you ladies that we are breaking camp tomorrow. We must go back down the mountain, get madam completely well, and leave before the winter storm comes."

"Oh, Rajendra Man, do we have to?" Gloria sounded like a six-year-old not ready to leave the party.

I, on the other hand, felt like I had taken another blow to my chest. So I wouldn't make it to the top after all. I looked up at the dim outline of the mountain above us. It seemed as out of my reach as the stars.

*   *   *

I leaned on Gloria for most of our downward journey. I shuffled past the Buddhist temple with the great staring eyes. The prayer flags flapped and bounced on their lines, and I stopped to watch their dance, hoping again that their prayers would float off to heaven.

"Tired, hon?" Gloria stopped with me, her arm securely round my waist.

I shook my head. All the restless desire that had driven me upward—and into my fever—had drained away. Now I was just there, almost down from the mountain, standing in front of another Buddhist temple, looking at my friend. Her face was gleaming with sweat. She was perfect.

"Your next teacher is already at your side," Madame Samsara had said. And what else? Something about the practice of love as the path.

Gloria! It was Gloria that Madame Samsara had meant all along. And the Light wasn't an experience to be found on the mountaintop, after all. No. It permeated everything: the earth, our cells, the firefly's glow, the moon as it comes into sight, the sun as it sets, the bright powdered snow. And the stories told by a friend who was patiently stroking my hair and willing me back to health.

I nodded toward the prayer flags, Gloria's *spider web for the gods*. "Looks like it's on the flight plan, after all," I said.

"Ah!" She grinned and studied the web. And then, of course, she giggled.

In a profound sense every man
has two halves to his being;
he is not one person so much as
two persons trying to act in unison.
I believe that in the heart of each human being
there is something which I can only
describe as a child of darkness
who is equal and complementary
to the more obvious child of light.

— Laurens van der Post
*The Dark Eye in Africa*
(1955)

# CHAPTER TEN

# Dawning of the Light Age

An age is called Dark,
not because the light fails to shine
but because people refuse to see it.

— James Michener
*Space*
(1982)

The woman in the seat beside me was fast asleep, her head bowed forward, her chin almost resting on her chest. Shortly after takeoff, she and I had raised our complimentary glass of champagne to each other and toasted our good fortune at getting bumped up to first class for the flight to Tokyo. But then she had pulled out a yellow legal pad and begun writing notes at a furious pace. Her pencil scratching annoyed me, so I had turned to my guidebook for Japan, only glancing back at my neighbor when the pencil sounds suddenly ceased. She was asleep. I was already missing Gloria's company. Gloria, my daring and darling friend, had flown out a day earlier to be back at work in Berkeley before the weekend.

"Darn!" I said to myself. I'd been hoping my next teacher was already at my side. As I suppressed a giggle at my own joke, the flight attendant appeared at my elbow.

"Enjoying the flight?" he asked. When I nodded, he said. "I'm Ted, your first-class flight attendant for today, no pun intended. You're stopping over in Japan!" he added, noticing my guidebook. "That's been my home base for the last year. I love it. You *must* go see the Ice Festival in Sapporo. You'll be arriving just in time. A quick side trip up to the north island, then?"

"Oh, no," I groaned. "I'm dying to get home."

"Miss your husband?" Ted glanced at my wedding ring and nodded sympathetically. "I know what you mean."

He was right. My longing to be with John had become a palpable ache.

"Well," Ted chirped, "see if it works out. You can't really lose, can you? A lovely side trip and then home? But, here—would you like a magazine? Nothing like a little news to distract you." And he added a glossy American weekly to the stack of reading material in my lap. "And please let me know if you need anything else—"

"How about another glass of champagne?" My neighbor was awake as suddenly as she had fallen asleep. "Since you're here," she added, smiling up at him.

He smiled back. "Certainly. Ladies, I'll be right back." And he was gone.

"I mean, why not?" My neighbor gave me a conspiratorial grin. "It's not a workday, now, is it?"

"No, it's not for me, at least. Though you seemed to be hard at work a while ago." I picked up the yellow pad that had slid off her lap and presented it to her.

"Force of habit," she admitted. "I can't think if I'm not scribbling." She extended her hand. "Dorothy Schoenfeld.

Pleased to meet you." Her grip was firm, as decisive as her tone of voice.

"Same here, Dorothy; I'm Jude, just Jude. What brings you to the East?"

"I've been digging up dirt," she said with a hearty laugh. "Literally! I'm an archaeologist. I've been at work in India for the last eight months. And you?"

"Eight months in India! Wow. And I've just been moaning about how long I've been away from home! It's only been about one month. I guess you could say I've been digging too, though not in the dirt exactly. I've been …" how could I put it? "…following the trail of some insights about, well…" I paused. It seemed too personal, but since we were perfect strangers, and I was never going to see her again, I felt safe in adding, "Lately, a couple of people have called me a 'spiritual anthropologist."

"Why then, our careers are kissing cousins!"

"Oh, it's not my career," I protested. "It's only my avocation."

"Ah, your *avocation*. How wonderful." Now she sounded like a professor. "An avocation. From the Latin, *a* plus *vocare*, you know—it's that thing that 'calls you away' from your ordinary life. Sound familiar?" She noticed my look of surprised recognition, then went on: "But, oh, how quickly that *avocation* can transform into your *vocatio*," another Latin word, "your *vocation*, an irrefutable summons to plunge deeper into your life, to fill your life with what you love—oops!" she stopped herself. "There I go again; quoting Latin derivations to someone I've just met. Occupational hazard, you know. You can take the professor out of the classroom, but you can't take the classroom out of the professor."

I hadn't initially sized her up correctly and now I tried again. She was so talkative, my instincts told me to back off. But there was nowhere to retreat to.

Then Ted reappeared with two flutes of champagne. "Cheers, ladies! Enjoy the flight!"

Dorothy and I toasted one another a second time. I couldn't believe the contrast, from campfire-brewed soup in the mountains of Nepal two days ago to French champagne on a luxury airliner now. And with a compulsive talker. "So, Dorothy," I had to ask, "did that happen to you?"

"Did what happen?"

"Did your *avocation* become your *vocation*?"

"Yes, yes, yes! It certainly did. Shall I tell you all about it?" She turned as far toward me as her seat belt allowed.

"Please." I smiled back, hiding my reservations about where the next hours were going. But as my body warmed from drinking champagne, I was sliding into a deep sense of contentment and surrender. I thought about how each of the people I'd met so far had offered information, an experience, or an insight that had changed my perspective on the world, on what holds us together and what pulls us apart. Now I sat beside Dorothy and listened for the lessons I hoped she would bring me. I was determined to make the most of it.

She had first traveled to South America, she began, as an exchange student in high school. "Oh, that was a time!" she said. Straight out of a large urban school in Chicago, she had landed in a small Peruvian town, unable to speak Spanish, fearful of the unfamiliar foods, the insects, just about everything. "And then, over the course of that summer, I fell in love. First with the family I was staying with, and then with the place, the people, the culture. And so after that first experience, I kept going back, earning money during the school year so that I could return every summer."

"Finally, in college," she continued, "I went on my first dig. Well, the first day I got to get down in the dirt, I felt like I'd come home. You know what I mean?" But she didn't pause for a reply. "More at home there than any place else I'd ever been. I began to wonder if I could make my passion my life. I didn't know it yet, but I had found my occupation, that activity that 'seizes hold' of you and won't let you go."

Dorothy took a deep breath and went on to the next chapter of her autobiography. "And that's it, really. Years in the field, a doctoral dissertation, and here I am—tenured. Imagine! Working at the University of Chicago, where I'm close to my aging mom, when I'm not with *mia mamá* in Peru, and happy as a clam. Well, except I've never liked the winters. And now I'm branching out, with a colleague, to Southeast Asia...so you never know. You, for example, were 'called away' to—where did you say you've been on this trip?"

I'd been looking around the cabin. "I didn't. Egypt, Syria, India, Nepal, and now Japan." I was getting frustrated with Dorothy. She talked too much and didn't listen. I thought of the boring hours ahead. I could tell she was clueless.

"There!" she was saying. "Called away. Far away from your everyday life to all these adventures. But what you've found just might 'seize hold' of you and become a 'summons' to a life devoted to such discoveries! Hmm? How does that sound?"

"Like a gift to God's ears!" That was an expression I hadn't heard, let alone used, in years. Realizing her insistent monologue was pushing my buttons, I laughed. "And it's a little breathtaking. Tell me more. What is it that you like best about your work?"

"My hands in the dirt," she answered without hesitation. She was beginning to tap her pencil. "Handling that dirt as though it were fine china. Touching it as it deserves to be touched, like sacred ground. And then—you know, you learn all about different civilizations in school, but when you go there, and you touch utensils that human beings long, long before you held as part of their daily life…well! Past and present collapse into one. I've spent long hours imagining what it must have been like to be an Incan or an Aztec during the heyday of their civilizations.

"And then, of course," now she grimaced, "I've spent just as long hours imagining the seizing of their lands by European conquerors and the subduing of their peoples…the elimination of their cultures…just a little over five hundred years ago."

I smoothed my hair back with one hand in an effort to get control of my reaction. "I remember what I was taught," I said. "Those cultures just seemed so…so different. So foreign and so far away. A lot like India and Egypt, I guess. Until I actually got there."

"That's it, isn't it! We've been taught that the First Nations peoples were 'pagan' and 'barbaric.' But that's because it's *convenient* to look at them in this way. It diminishes our own barbarism. We push stories that emphasize their violence rather than their sophistication. And it's all too easy to use our engineering accomplishments as measuring sticks. Many conclude that by comparison, other nations, other times, were not as 'developed' as ours. But my studies have convinced me that the Incas, Mayas, Aztecs—they were not backward at all." She tapped her pad with the eraser end of her pencil for emphasis.

"Ready for lunch, ladies?" Ted was back. Trays laden with full-course meals, complete with finger bowls in which fresh mint leaves floated, arrived with a swoop. Dorothy dug in. I picked at my pasta, thinking about my own assumptions about the Central and South American Indians. The images in my mind were fairly primitive. The pictures of the ruined cities on the tops of mountains had always remained just that in my mind—pictures. I wanted to gaze deeper into it than that and maybe Dorothy could help.

"The Incas," I began, "they worshiped the sun, didn't they?" I didn't have to say much to get her going again. For, clearly, she was better at talking than listening.

"So glad you asked!" She wiped her mouth and turned toward me again. The gold flecks in her eyes were sparkling. "I have come to see the Incas as the ultimate children of the sun. Theirs was a magnificent sun kingdom, really, which they glorified with gold. They built glittering temples." She seemed to be reassuring me. "When you've caught a glimpse of their lives, even what little remains, it's just so fascinating."

I was fidgeting in my seat. I couldn't get comfortable. "I've been thinking a lot about sun worship," I said keeping the conversation in my court. "It's actually been a big part of the focus of this trip. And what I'm wondering is…was worship of the sun itself all there was to it? When we refer to it simply as 'sun worship,' are we missing something else that we might need to know?" If I had to listen to her, I told myself, I might as well get something useful out of it.

She lifted her tray in Ted's direction, and as he took it she answered, "Great question! Now, we have to be very careful here not to interpret a culture we can't really know. We can only interpret it based on what we know of our own. But that would just be more cultural imperialism. So I wouldn't want to pretend that I have access to all the wisdom and the secret knowledge to which the Incas had access but that is lost to us." *Tap tap*. She'd picked up her pad and pencil again. "However," her voice dropped into a confidential tone and she looked straight into my eyes, "however, we have found texts declaring that for the Incas there was One more powerful than the sun. To convey what this One was, they covered one wall inside some of their temples with gold—but the very center of that golden wall was always left empty. And these temples, these walls, were located precisely so that on the winter solstice south of the equator, the rays from what they called the Living Burning Light would shine on the empty place in the wall."

"But weren't those just the rays of the sun?" I asked. "What's the difference between that and flat-out sun worship?" I was hoping my question would lead her to reveal something more.

"Ah," she said, "notice that a portion of the wall was *empty*. See what a powerful message that is? The empty wall shows that they believed the highest source was formless. Without material body. With this understanding comes the insight that everything that has ever been created—every name, form, image, or body…absolutely *everything* comes out of this unformed source that they called the Living Burning Light. That source is not prejudiced toward any group, person, or culture in particular. Because it created them all! It is our human nature to try to name and interpret all that has been created." We were practically nose to nose by now. "And it is our human failing so often to declare erroneously which things are of a lesser or greater value."

A thought came into my mind. *Our human nature, and our human failing.* I momentarily closed my eyes and let this thought ripple back through my memories of all I had experienced, all I had learned so far on my trip. One thing seemed clear. It was not only individuals like Akhenaten and Moses, or Ezekiel and Paul, who had understood that the sun, or light itself, was a symbol for the Divine Light. Whole civilizations the world over had known it, too.

But Dorothy was still talking. "After the solstice sun had shone on the empty golden wall, giving the Incas life and light, a high priest would don his golden diadem and golden sandals and sacrifice a white llama. During their sacrifices, the priests would turn the faces of those about to be offered toward the sun."

*Of course!* I thought. Of course the Inca priests turned their sacrificial victims toward the sun. They knew that they would experience the Pure Light at their death. While Dorothy wasn't the kind of person I'd go out of my way to meet, with her pencil tapping and constant note taking, by now I had to admit I was learning something. Maybe I just needed to relax and let go. Maybe I was being petty.

I leaned forward. By now I was really interested in what she was saying. "What about the Aztecs?" I asked.

"The Aztecs and Mayans who lived in Mexico and on the Yucatán Peninsula were the cousins of the Incas," she replied. "They also built great, tall pyramids to the sun. Their principal god was Quetzalcoatl, who was represented by the planet Venus, the morning star. Eagles and serpents were part of their lore, too."

"That's incredible!" We were getting somewhere. Now, I was tapping my guidebook as Dorothy tapped her pad. I had a personal insight. Both the Buddha and Jesus had had something to say about the morning star. And the serpent and the eagle, were solar symbols used the world over, well, practically since the beginning of civilization; Bill's lessons stood by me. Dorothy nodded at me, her eyes bright. "And one more thing about the Aztecs…" she cocked her head "…they believed that their deceased eventually entered the fire, or the house of the sun, in the lowest region of the universe. From there people would be sent back to earth."

"Like reincarnation for the Hindus and the Buddhists?"

"Something like that."

And then I had another revelation. Isn't this also like the near-death experience? In NDEs, those who face death travel toward a light or a fire. And then they return to tell about it. My dreams of the Light, so long ago now, seemed immediate again.

Dorothy glanced down at the cover of the magazine sitting on the stack on my lap. "Hmm," she said. "See this picture of the good guys in light hats and the bad guys in the dark hats?"

"Yeah." The magazine cover was illustrating another "Wild West Week" for the U.S. economy. "They're trying to say something here about who's in control, right? The guys in the white hats."

"No doubt," she agreed. "But, really, this sort of imagery comes right out of antiquity, portraying who is right or wrong by the colors they wear. It's right out of the old myths that describe the sun defeating the darkness. These associations go back...well, certainly, back to the Sumerians. And the earliest written records. Ancient *Zoroastrian* beliefs about the Light and the Dark are an inseparable part of our thinking today."

I grinned and scribbled down the name.

"Zoroaster, or Zarathustra," Dorothy said, "was the founder of a dualistic religion about 3,000 years ago. Scholars have a field day debating the dates, but, anyway, he lived as a prophet and religious leader in the area that is now Iran. It all started for him with a vision of God—"

"Of course!" I flashed on Moses and Akhenaten and their "visions." For some reason, I also stretched and looked around to see if anyone else in first class was listening to our conversation.

Dorothy was still going on, she obviously loved listening to herself talk. "He believed that we humans must make a choice between the forces of good and those of evil. Basically, Zoroastrians believe that the cosmos is a battleground between the Spirit of Light and the Spirit of Darkness. And we're still pretty hung up on looking at the world this way. Black or white. How often do you still hear that? And just look at your magazine. It's all over the media, too. Always has been. We love to make things simple. But," her pencil began tapping again as if underscoring each word she was saying, "but this way of seeing can be incredibly destructive."

"Wow. Strong words. How so?" Although I was feeling somewhat annoyed by Dorothy, I knew what was coming next was important.

She was precise. "Why must we always see things as being in opposition to each other?" Her frustration rang in her voice. "I think that's stifling. And it can feed prejudice and discrimination. It often leads to injustice! Good versus bad, dark versus light, right versus left, male versus female. It's always one thing against the other. It's too bad we base so much of our day-to-day lives on this dualistic way of thinking. Darkness is as important in our experience as light. They go together."

"Oh. My. God!" It struck me like a bolt from the sky. "I see what you're saying. These things are tandem realities; they're *complementary* rather than separate and at war with each other. What would happen if we really grasped that?" The thought rattled me. I had been so focused on the Light—had this focus been too narrow? Why hadn't I thought of this? Those near-death experiences almost always involve a great light surrounded by an equally profound darkness.

Dorothy gave a triumphant nod. "Exactly. And what about 'dark matter'—the matter that scientists have discovered within the darkness? Still, you don't have to be a scientist, or an archaeologist, to know that great treasures lie in the dark. Think of the seed sprouting in dark soil and the creativeness of fertility. Think of our dreams... of our brains refueling in the night. Think of our earliest life in the womb." Her voice became softer. "Without the darkness, the light cannot shine so brightly. In fact, without it there would be no perception of light at all. Dark and light are simply different aspects of *one* reality. You might say God is just like electrical energy: sometimes you see it—the light, that is—and sometimes you don't, and that's the darkness. But you should know it's always there." *Tap. Tap.*

"Are you suggesting that God is both the Darkness and the Light?"

"Maybe." She smiled. "Maybe that's closer to the truth. You know...in the same way every wavelength of light has a tandem and inseparable dark wave."

And with that, she picked up her pad and began scribbling at breakneck speed.

I leaned my head against the back of my seat and felt the imagery that I had been hoarding all this time begin to expand. I mentally walked back through all the events of my journey including the dark moments plunging me toward despair at Varanasi. Now, too, I recognized darkness as my ally in the creative inspiration that enabled me to connect the dots between Moses and Akhenaten. Darkness had been with me and my companion all along. Darkness had held me gently. What I sorely needed was to embrace it in the same way I welcomed Light. Over and over again I had been shown an eternal essence that spanned time and space. I had experienced that connection between light and dark! Could I say, then—but without that "cultural imperialism" Dorothy had warned me about—that there was a single unifying agent within all religious systems, past and present?

*I'd been the one not listening.* The insight seemed to rise up from the depths of a dark, dark sea teeming with life, up to a surface gleaming in the sun. Vocatio, I thought. A spiritual summons, indeed.

How is one to live a moral and compassionate existence when one finds darkness not only in one's culture but within oneself?
There are simply no answers to some of the great pressing questions.
You continue to live them out, making your life a worthy expression
of leaning into the light.

— Barry Lopez,
*Arctic Dreams*
(1968)

# CHAPTER ELEVEN

# Gateway to Light

"From which angle
do we view the Light;
Are we enlightened from
our culture's receptiveness,
Or from within?"

— Anonymous

Again, my bleary eyes opened to new surroundings. I was in a *ryokan*, or guesthouse, near the Tokyo airport. This was a scheduled overnight layover before the long flight to California. Rice-paper *shoji* screens surrounded me, and beneath the futon I was lying on lay thin *tatami* floor mats. It had been a short night's sleep. If I was going to make my flight, I needed to get up. I pulled the heavy down comforter up to my ears.

But...Ted. Darn him. "You have to go see the Ice Festival in Sapporo." The flight attendant's suggestion kept ringing in my mind. I lay still, wondering why I felt drawn to yet another diversion when I was longing to go home. Hokkaido, the north island, is Japan's land of ice and snow. Hadn't I had enough ice and snow in the Himalayas?

And then, thinking about the mountains, I began thinking about Gloria, with her lust for life and how much she relished new experiences. "One vote for yes," I said aloud. Then I counted up all my temporary gurus—Rick, Bill, Huda, Muhammad, Father Luke, Madame Samsara, Dorothy. I was sure each one would say, "Go." Rishi was a harder call. I guessed he would shrug and look indifferent if I asked for his vote, but I was pretty clear that, deep down, he would give it. Another yes, then.

And John?

I buried my face under the comforter. I could almost smell my husband's sweat-damp skin, could almost feel him reaching for me, could almost hear him whisper, "Go." John, too, would understand.

"Okay, okay," I muttered. "It's unanimous. Surely I can justify one final detour." I was resolute as I stood up. "I'm going to the Ice Festival."

*   *   *

I was in Sapporo by mid-afternoon and immediately mesmerized by its blanket of snow glittering in the last rays of the setting sun. Rainbows bounced off ice crystals in every direction. My new lodging was in the center of the city, an easy walk to the International Ice Festival. Pots of boiling broth beckoned from the crowded food stalls. I resisted, though, and slipped into a small, warm shop, where I immediately felt oversized. Muttering a meek, "Hai," which I believed meant "yes," I pointed to the plastic facsimile of Hokkaido Ramen on display. Within minutes, I was slurping my noodles and feeling the steam wafting toward my face and through my hair.

Everything would be all right.

Fed and refreshed, I rounded the corner to the main plaza, where a barren persimmon tree stood stark against the dusky sky. Snowflakes drifted down onto the stage of the International Ice Festival in a whitewashed belt of frozen space between the boulevards. The size of the crowd was startling. Some people were hard at work cleaning and manicuring blocks of ice; others were watching the work, talking, taking pictures. People were in constant motion among the maze of creations. From where I stood, I could see ice bears, whales, cranes, fish, replicas of famous statues from around the world and a *torii* gate made entirely of ice and more than two stories high. For the next hour I mingled with the crowd in the corridors between the sculptures, watching their creators give ongoing care to the ever-changing shapes. Artists and craftspeople from around the globe were there—teams from Thailand, New Zealand, Australia, Korea, China, Finland, Malaysia, Indonesia, Italy, and America. Something exciting was percolating in the raw air. I could feel it, but I couldn't name it.

In truth, I was too tired—too tired to think, to analyze, to move. The hotel offered an *ofuro* bath, a hearty meal, and at last a long, peaceful sleep.

\* \* \*

At the very heart of the festival's displays stood the massive torii gate ice sculpture I'd seen the day before. The crowds were thinner this afternoon, so I could get closer to watch a Japanese man in a down snowsuit, chainsaw in hand, finishing his repairs on a section. Still breathing hard, he was looking up at the top of the gate. The steam of his breath condensed into droplets that caught on his chin and froze into pearls of ice as I watched.

"Excuse me, please, sir," I started as delicately as I could. "I am admiring this magnificent gate. Is it your creation?"

We had noticed each other the day before during my tour of the sculptures, and I'd been drawn back again today to stop and watch. He took a long look at me. Only then came a smile and a bow.

"This is a collectively planned and executed project," he replied. "It has taken twenty-one days to construct. Many weeks have gone into the planning, many enjoyable weeks. Each day we cut and lift the ice. I oversee the work and provide artistic or aesthetic help, final shaping and detailing. I am, I must say, at last happy with what I see. It is easy, comparatively, to plan in such scale, but the execution of the project is more difficult. Physical reality is unlike the scale of the mind. This year our progress has been well-timed and the work has been almost easy. We are satisfied that we have pleased the *kami*."

"The kami?"

"The spirit-god that inhabits everything in the physical world," he explained. "In rocks, in rivers, in trees, in everything. In all nature, the spirit-god is present. The torii, the gate, has been built to honor the kami. It fulfills a very specific purpose."

"Yes..." My voice trailed off as my eyes followed his gaze at the gate.

"Perhaps, if I may suggest, madam…" I nodded and he went on. "If you will squint your eyes for a moment and invite all your concentration. Now look through the gate, well beyond."

Without question or resistance, I did as I was told. I narrowed my eyes and let the din of our surroundings fade away, and then I waited.

I waited for the next words of my new guide.

"Now," he said after a long while. "Visualize that you have just entered the first of three torii standing in a row. You see them all, but you are present only at the first. Pass slowly, very slowly, under the first of these gates. As you do, you will find the purpose is to cleanse your heart and mind.

"There is a thatched-roof building ahead of you. It is the house of the kami. Look about you. People are strolling outside the shrine. They are merry, even in the cold. It is morning with its fresh new light, the happiest time of day. Can you see the pilgrims washing their hands and rinsing their mouths in order to purify themselves before they pray? Look carefully. You can see it!"

I did see it. I almost laughed with pleasure.

"Good. Now move closer and enter the mouth of the shrine. Watch the faithful approach. Hear them clapping. Can you see them pulling the rope attached to a clapper in the ceiling?"

I nodded.

"The sound calls the god's attention. Pilgrims are now bowing and praying silently. Please, carefully, notice the Shinto priests near you. They are wearing tall, black, lacquered hats and carrying pine sprigs. Perhaps they are waving the branches. From time to time, you are greeted with eye contact from a curious worshipper. You hear the constant clapping of flat hands. You see the small offer- ings of rice cakes and vegetables. Become aware of the strips of white paper prayers meticulously folded and tied into knots."

I nodded. His voice sounded almost mechanical now, and yet the images were vibrant and bright.

"Now, turn back and look out the mouth of the shrine. Look to where you have come from. This is the East. Trace the radiance that has brought you to this spot. Patience, clarity, and non-attachment must engulf one here. If you are patient enough, you will see the trail of your own existence. For you have moved not on human feet but have made a journey of the spirit."

There was a pause. Then he spoke again, slowly and softly: "This is the Land of the Rising Sun. From where you stand, and far past the furthest point that your exis- tence allows you to know, there the sun has always risen."

After a pause, his voice came as a command. "Now come back to the first torii!"

The man was still standing before me, his hands clasped, his eyes closed, the chain saw placed some dis- tance away on the frozen ground. What power did he have that I had given myself over so easily to following his story, to seeing what I did not know and had not experienced?

He opened his eyes and spoke again. "This world needs its stories. The torii is the perch where the mythical cock heralded the dawn and brought *Amaterasu*, the Sun Goddess, from her cave. Amaterasu Omikami is the supreme Shinto deity—"

"But aren't you Buddhist, too?" I interrupted, and then wished I hadn't. If I was disturbed by how easily I had engaged with this stranger in his...visualization? Meditation? Trip? What was it?—now I was equally frustrated by my need to feel in control.

"Of course," the man smiled at me. "We remain faithful to both simultaneously. We find it very easy to cross over between Shinto and Buddhism in our lives. We are born and marry Shinto, and then we die Buddhist."

"But, but...doesn't this trouble you? Isn't it confusing?" And a thought came to me. *Oh, Jude, enough already with the "black-and-white" answers.*

The man's smile deepened. "It is neither troubling nor confusing, madam, not in the least. Most honored households have both Shinto and Buddhist shrines and hold to both beliefs. There is less suffering when duality does not reign. Nature is not dual, not good or evil. It *exists*. It has existed, and it will exist. We are taught simply to stay pure, to follow true impulses of our hearts."

Then he spoke more slowly again, as if to carve his words in my mind: "God does not have a religion. God does not speak a language. God does not have a culture. It is we humans who require these things."

The wooden shoes of a trio of women suddenly struck an odd tune on the ice. Their formal kimonos, their faces painted with pale makeup, their elaborate coiffures, and the red box that each one carried carefully before her—all these things set the trio apart from the rest of the visitors, and yet they seemed to add just the variety the scene required. They paused before the torii and then looked in our direction and bowed. We bowed back.

The engineer-artist-believer held out his gloved hand and let the snowflakes fall on it; each flake glistening for a moment, then disappearing. He watched transfixed for several silent minutes.

"They are each so precious," he said when he looked at me again. "Everything in nature, like all of us, is unique. There is light in each. All are different, yet each possesses the essence of the same." He bowed very slowly toward me.

And in that moment, looking at this down-clad stranger framed by his massive, frozen sculpture, I had my vision...the one I had been longing for. Though it was nothing like what I had expected.

I saw the world as a web of intertwined beliefs, each elaborated by the separate cultures, peoples, and times of its believers, yet all beliefs valid beyond their specific times and places. Each strand was as strong and vital to the web as a whole. The web was shining, every strand gleaming and golden within a common element. A common ground resolved in unity. The Light.

Slowly, slowly, I bowed. "*Domo arigato.*" I had learned how to say just one thing in Japanese: "Thank you very much."

And I turned back toward the hotel.

Is the person who is able to see the power in many beliefs, in one, and in none, on the verge of metamorphosis? I wondered about that. Has this process already begun, here, in the Land of the Rising Sun? And in other lands and cultures, too? Aren't many people already living their lives this way, in the peaceful, conscious coexistence of beliefs? Is such a thing all that shocking? Is it all that unique? Or did I need to learn this for another reason? My thoughts opened like an enormous flower.

"Rick!" I almost called his name aloud as I remembered the conversation that had set me on this journey.

I was ready to go home.

A light there is in the beyond
which makes the Creator
visible to the creature,
who only in beholding Him
finds peace.

— Dante Alighieri
*The Divine Comedy*
(*ca.* 1308-1321)

# CHAPTER TWELVE

# A New Vision: Life in the Light

Someday perhaps the inner light
will shine forth from us,
and then we'll need no other light.

— Johann Wolfgang von Goethe
*Elective Affinities*
(1854)

Traffic had been stop-and-go ever since I'd emerged from the Marin Tunnel. I had just visited Rick again, and now the freeway ahead was jammed all the way around the curve and down to the Golden Gate Bridge.

Had the Bay Area streets grown more crowded during the weeks I had been away? And what was causing the slowdown this time? An accident? The weather? A blowing rain was raising whitecaps on the bay, which was a dull gray today instead of its usual blues and greens. I would be late for my reunion with Bill.

Still, I was grateful for the warmth and comfort of my car. And, besides, who could beat the view? Even on the gloomiest of days, San Francisco rises like Oz from the waters around it, a blend of natural and manmade beauty. This was my first trip to the city since my return a week ago, and now the skyline took my breath away. I felt like I was seeing it for the first time.

"Om Sweet Om," I thought, and laughed out loud. "*Ommmmmmm.*" I tried imitating Madame Samsara's throaty hum, but it only made me laugh even harder.

Yet it was true. It was so sweet to be home. If I were to paint a picture of my home, I would place the radiant source of light right here with my friends, my family, my home. I let the images of my homecoming flash past my inner eye as I shifted in and out of gear, inching forward on the highway...remembering recent conversations.

\*    \*    \*

"You look even more beautiful," John had declared.

I was standing at the kitchen sink, drinking a huge glass of water and plucking at the plants on the windowsill. "Photosynthesis," I was thinking, marveling at the veins that filled even the smallest leaves. He and I had just walked in the door from the airport, and I was dazed—dazzled, really, by the ordinary, extraordinary sight of home. I turned to him with what must have been a goofy smile.

"It's true," he told me. "There's more light in your eyes."

And I had walked across the room to hold him and be held. Not in my imagination during a phone call, but wrapped in the bony, sinewy circle of his very real arms.

Over the next few days, I had told him everything

I had seen and heard and felt. He'd raised his eyebrows a time or two when I spoke about my inexplicable brief intoxication with "guru" Muhammad and my redemptive visit to the old Syriac church.

"Well," said my husband, "let's hope that never happens again!" Then he mimed locking the door and throwing away the key. So I mimed retrieving it, flinging open the door, and grabbing his hand.

"I can promise you it will not happen again," I said, looking deep into his eyes. "I've learned that lesson. *Don't mistake the messenger for the message.*" Still holding his hand, I added, "So many lessons...I feel...more awake. Do you know what I mean? The things I saw and heard, the whole trip—it woke me up!" I was struggling to express what can probably not be put into words.

John gazed at me for a long moment. The playful expression he usually wore had dropped into something deeper and more relaxed. "So now the question is," he said slowly, "how will we let this change *us*? How do we live that message? How do we live what you've—what *we've* learned?"

But when I went to see Rick, he couldn't resist teasing me. Oh, he had listened carefully and seriously enough, but at the end of my long story, his first words had been, "So! You think you're going to turn me into a theist after all, don't you?" The cats, who had nestled against our legs, one for each of us, as we sat on his overstuffed sofas, raised their heads as though to hear my answer to his question.

I had shrugged. "We'll have to see; won't we?"

And he and I just grinned at each other.

Gloria, I'd been amazed to learn when I phoned her, was still jet-lagged. My friend who had taken the hop from Delhi to San Francisco in her long, capable stride was now having trouble keeping her head off her desk at work. We laughed at the irony of it, for I had taken her advice and tried to synchronize my exposure to sunlight and darkness during my first few days back, so I was in pretty good shape. Her energy returned as she pumped me for all the details of the rest of my journey. "Mmm… mm-hmm," she punctuated my tale much as she had during my call from Damascus.

And then she broke in just as suddenly. "Jude! It's all so clear! We've got to follow up!" I heard her opening her map drawer with a jolt. "So where do we go next!" It was more a proclamation than a question.

"Gloria, Glo-ri-a!" I had to laugh. "Girlfriend, if any-one taught me that I don't need to go halfway around the world to find the teacher I need, it's you."

She was quiet for a moment. "And vice versa, Jude, vice versa."

There we were, on opposite ends of the phone line, basking in a warmth that would have been gushy had it not been so palpable.

"You know," she said at last, "this change in you is so…so great."

"What do you mean 'change'?" I asked, hoping she would put it into words for me.

She pretended to be frustrated. "I told you before!"

"You did? When?"

"After your visit to Samsara. Right away, I noticed this calmness about you. Even when you were sick in the mountains, it was still there, but I feel it even more now. You were just so preoccupied you don't remember me saying so."

\* \* \*

A blare of car horns interrupted my reminiscing and brought me back to the traffic jam of the present. "Ah!" I exclaimed, à la Gloria. Distracted by my daydreams, I had let a little space open up ahead of me, and the drivers behind me were protesting. Still beaming from my memories, I shifted into gear and began to move forward. "Well," I congratulated myself, "I can certainly handle heavy traffic better, anyway."

And then I jammed my palm on the horn. Darting up out of my blind spot, a car was trying to cut into my lane. "What are you trying to do?" I caught myself yelling. But then I let him in. The guy needed space, too. But he only stared straight ahead. I had a vision of the chaos Muhammad and I had witnessed on the banks of the Nile—carts and cars, drivers and pedestrians, all in the noisy cacophony of Egyptian life.

My impatience, that old friend, although less harsh now, was still with me. Yes, I still had some work to do.

\* \* \*

Outside and under the bright sun, away from his lair, the staff lounge and reserve stacks, Bill seemed awkward and out of place. The sunlight, streaming through rain clouds, made him blink. I had coaxed him into coming out with me for a cappuccino to celebrate the end of my journey. Now he sat looking around the café as though taking notes. I watched the barista make our cappuccinos, ladling on the froth. Her gestures reminded me of the care that had gone into the ritual pouring of the coffee at Muhammad and Leila's home.

Finally I turned back to Bill. "Did you get my postcards?"

He was absentmindedly drumming on the table as though still at his keyboard, "Yes, uh, yes! Focus, William," he muttered. I hid my grin behind my steaming cup. "And your emails, too," he added. "Very gratifying, very provoking. Provoking thought, I mean."

"You are the one who provoked my thinking," I told him. "I'm here today especially to thank you for making my trip such an enlightening experience." The whole of it…without Bill's lesson on symbols, I would have missed a lot.

"This is not the end of the journey, Jude," he replied. I recognized that schoolteacher tone. "Not the end, not at all. This is the gold of the philosopher's stone, the alchemist's dream. This journey merely connects to another. You've discovered a philosophy, and now you're off on another journey. It will take you—who knows where?" He tapped his temple. "But perhaps you don't yet know about this new journey." Though his voice was gentle, his bright blue eyes were as eager as ever.

I smiled and shook my head. "Not really. Not quite. Maybe you can tell me. Do you know where all this is going?"

"Good question," he said. "Good question! The truth

of the matter is, I've been preparing for your return. Your insights, you see." He looked around at the neighboring tables and his voice dropped into a conspiratorial whisper. "They inspired me to do some more investigating." He grinned. "I sat down and put the old noggin to work, and I thought 'why, certainly other people throughout the ages must have been aware of the Light'—the Light in the way that we mean it, as the Divine, the Holy One, the Ultimate Source, Energy, God…you know, all of the above. In the last, say, five thousand years, there simply had to be other souls who left behind a legacy that might reveal their own experience of it, their ruminations of the Light. And where was that legacy to be found?" His eyes were sparkling. "Well it's not only in the near-death experience stuff. That's our modern-day fixation with it. Ha!" He slapped the table and turned around as though to grab a book off a shelf. He looked stunned to find a window overlooking the bay instead of shelves. He sat still for an instant.

Then he whipped around so quickly he almost overturned his chair. "Where? Why, in their books and memoirs, of course! It would show up in their plays, in their stories, in their writings, in their art, their parables and their visions. And guess what, Jude?" He waited.

"What?" I leaned forward. It was like we were playing a delightful but serious game.

"It has! It has shown up." Bill thrust himself back, clasped his hands on his belly, and started to launch his feet onto the table. "Oh, heavens, William! Public manners!" His feet came down with a thump.

Every gesture seemed dear and familiar to me.

Another homecoming. I remembered how overwhelmed I had felt during my first meeting with him. Now I couldn't wait to hear what he had to say.

He began again. "Of course these individuals did not call what they had found the 'Light,' as we are doing today. There were too many obstacles. For the most part, you see, they encountered it individually. They had no context, no cross-cultural references, no reports of near-death experiences."

*Just like me in the beginning*, I thought, but Bill was still going. "They didn't have dream laboratories and data banks with which to compare experiences."

"And no Madame Samsaras," I chimed in, "to read the Akashic Records. No Glorias to explain the physical phenomena.

"Yes, yes," Bill was delighted, "and no Muhammads, Dorothys, or Father Lukes! Those who went before us often had no way to substantiate what they had experienced because their experiences were so very personal in nature, so ineffable... indescribable. So they could only try, to the best of their abilities, try to create awareness of the Light in the manner best suited to their time their audience and their culture."

"Through art, then?" I asked, and Bill tapped the side of his nose and winked. "But this means they must have," I paused to think, "well, they must have disguised it, too. Right?"

"Some did, yes. Purposefully. While others, I think, weren't sure just what to call it. It is a terrible oppression, you know, not to be allowed to think for oneself, nor to hold a belief that differs from the status quo. Hmph!"

He scowled. "An oppression not unheard of today," he rumbled, glaring at his thumbs. "We're just more subtle about it now."

As I nodded, he looked back up from under those shaggy eyebrows: "Topic, William, stick to the topic." He cleared his throat. "So there was oppression, yes, but there was also limited access to other people's experiences and to information. And perhaps those who had the experience didn't want to tell others; maybe they wanted to hold onto it or hide behind closely guarded societies like the Freemasons or the Illuminati. Maybe they didn't feel the need for proof or validation and simply hid it in the context of city grids like Paris or the Vatican or in architecture, symbol, and statuary. Maybe in alchemy. Maybe they didn't really have the desire to spread the word. And then," he was glowering again, "these ideas might have been dangerous for them, yes? So, like the Holy Grail, they cloaked it in metaphor."

"Well," I suggested, "it seems to me that even now they might seem…well, controversial. Or, um, farfetched."

"Farfetched. Hmmm." He smiled and looked up, reading some unseen, private text on the café's ceiling. "Hmph!" He pulled himself back. "Nonetheless, I did stumble onto the writings of a number of individuals who, I believe, were urging us to seek the Light."

"Great—" I began, but he was already counting them off.

"Take, for instance, the venerable Plato, and then his follower Plotinus, who believed that the One—that's what he called the great Source—*the One* can only be known through an ecstatic experience. A mystical union. Well, yes, hmm, you heard all about that with Muhammad, didn't you. But Plato, now, Plato in the Allegory of the Cave…"

I leaned forward. I wanted to hear this.

"Well," he said, "here, let me tell you the story. You'll see for yourself: A group of men are trapped deep within a dark cave. A fearful existence. All their lives they are chained in the dark to that one spot. But one day one of the men gets free! He walks out of the cave and into a world of brilliant light. He sees. He feels. He hears— oh, and he tastes, and he smells, too. Let's throw in all the senses. Why not? He experiences all these beautiful things that he could not possibly have imagined down in the dark. A new awareness bursts upon him. It permeates his whole being. He feels completely changed by this experience."

Bill edged forward in his chair for emphasis, "And then, just as suddenly, he is thrust out of the lighted world and back into the cave. He tells the others, 'Listen! There's a world of light out there. And beautiful unknown things that you cannot imagine. I have seen them and touched them and tasted them.'" And so on.

"'What's that?' they say." Bill was growling now, acting out all the parts. "'What's that? How can that be? You're crazy!' In their lack of knowledge, you see, their lack of experience, these men cannot understand what he's saying. They don't believe him. He yearns for the lighted world again, but he's trapped. And the years go by, and go by, and gradually he, too, begins to believe that this great experience must have been a bizarre dream, an illusion. He resigns himself to the darkness. But he never forgets the dream, you see, he never forgets his dream of the lighted world."

"It's our life, isn't it?" I said. "The darkness. Human folly…"

"Oh, yes, oh, yes, *but*," he waggled a forefinger at me, "but I think it's even more than that. It's a story about the Light. The wondrous, beatific Light that we never quite forget, but which fades from our view, fades from our experience as we engage in our everyday lives. See? We have all, at one time, have been with the Light. But our preoccupations with what we call our lives have dimmed our memory. The Light is the truth we've forgotten. That's what Plato is telling us." He dropped back into his academic mode: "Plato is perhaps one of the most obvious places where a Light theology is presented and can be easily understood."

"Bravo!" I was applauding his performance as well as the ideas. Then, "So there are others?"

He took a breath. "I believe there's another great thinker who wrote about the Light. And within a traditional Catholic setting, in fact."

"Who was that?"

"Pierre Teilhard de Chardin." I wouldn't even attempt to imitate Bill's flawless French pronunciation as I repeated the name. "Born 1881, died 1955. Now, he didn't call it the Light, of course, how could he? Rather, he called it the Omega Point, that bright point toward which we are all evolving, where relationships will be in harmony and all consciousness integrated." He smiled. "Oh, yes, it was quite a modern idea. And what was this Omega Point? It was the Christ, *bien sûr.*" He answered his rhetorical question. "Yet here's the catch, my dear, here's the catch. The Omega Point and the Christ looked like the Light. Not Jesus, my dear. Teilhard de Chardin believed that the whole of creation is evolving in a single direction and will eventually burst forth into Light at its completion. He had to call this Light something else. His freedom of thought was curtailed. Everyone's was! His ideas were seen as controversial, and if he had called God the Light, as we are doing, there might have been all sorts of negative repercussions from the Church."

"So how did the Catholic Church respond?"

"Not well." Bill's lips turned down in an elaborate frown. "Though I suppose it could have been worse. The Holy Office advised all good Catholics to read him 'with caution.' Ha! I'll say! This is incendiary stuff if we take it really seriously." His face was ablaze.

"Wow." I nodded in amazement.

"You can say that again. And there's more!" He was on a roll now. This topic filled him with joy. "Dante, too. He pondered this mysterious Light." And he launched into a quote from the *Paradiso* without pausing for breath. "'A light there is in the beyond which makes the Creator visible to the creature, who only in beholding Him finds peace.' Or *her*, in beholding her," Bill added with a nod in my direction. "No point in not being gender inclusive. We know better now. Or then take Emanuel Swedenborg—"

"Who?" I was struggling to keep up with Bill's sweep through history and philosophy.

"Born in Stockholm in 1688. Contributed to various fields of natural science." Bill recited the facts as though he was reading an encyclopedia. "But late in life—whoa, slow down, William, slow down…not so late, why you're almost there yourself." He ran a hand through his salt-and-pepper hair as though to make sure it was still there. "In any case," he jump-started the story again, "Swedenborg had a religious crisis and proceeded to write vivid descriptions of his experiences. He described the 'Light of the Lord' as a Light of immeasurable brightness. And he believed that it permeated the hereafter.

"And there are moderns like Hira Ratan Manek, HMR for short, who profess no religious belief other than safe sun gazing—maybe this is what Akhenaten and Moses were actually doing? You know, it's plausible they were staring at the sun. And we can't forget Akbar the Great, the Indian Mughal emperor known for his religious curiosity. He abandoned the Muslim practice of praying toward Mecca in preference for facing the sun. You have to wonder what was going on with him too. My God—did we ever fully talk about the Great Pyramid? Mercy! Now there's the grand pillar of light written in stone."

He stopped abruptly, then almost mumbled, "I'm planning to do more research for you. I'll let you know what I find."

"Great! Shall we walk?" I was dying to get up and stretch. The intermittent rain had finally stopped, leaving a cool, clear evening in its wake. The lights of the East Bay were just coming on; the sky over the eastern hills reflected the sunset almost as if it were the dawn.

"I'm waxing poetic," I chided myself, smiling and pulling my jacket tighter.

We had almost reached my car in the bowels of the

Civic Center's garage when Bill stopped and turned to me again. "There's one more thing…"

I nodded and waited.

"It is predicted that we will reach the point where our fossil fuels will no longer be adequate to support life as we currently live it. You know, Peak Oil Theory and Global Warming, er…I mean Climate Change. And even if we don't run out altogether, the effects of global pollution and overpopulation will certainly force some change. Perhaps there is only a limited number of years before we peak out of these fuels, at which point, or before, let us hope that we will resort to a cleaner power source, perhaps solar. Are you with me?"

"Sure. But what does this have to do with—?"

"It may seem off the subject, but just hear me out." He looked young and eager, even in the ghastly fluorescent light of the parking garage. "Here we are in the new millennium. And the zodiac is moving, too. Yes, it's an ancient system, a symbolic system like all the rest. The zodiac is slowly moving into a new position in the heavens, an event that only occurs roughly every 2,000 years or so and a full cycle takes about 26,000 years."

"Are you talking about precession?" I asked him. "The shift that's supposed to bring in, finally, the so-called Age of Aquarius? Oh, come on, Bill, I thought we got over all that in the '60s!" I was teasing him. I couldn't quite believe the turn the conversation had taken.

"You are skeptical, of course. Good. Good. But what if there is something to it? There are cycles in all of human existence, you know, and every age has its new revelations and its own definite patterns. We are currently seeing shifts of some magnitude in multiple areas. Perhaps some of this signals a totally new cycle for humankind. The seeds for this new 'Aquarian' awareness are being sown in our time. I can't help but think the Light is part of that new pattern and will contribute to a spiritual evolution that might someday become widespread." He nodded vigorously.

"So, yes," he went on, "I do think it is significant that the Age of Aquarius is set to emerge fully at about the same time we peak out of fossil fuels, even if it takes another three hundred years. I'm just saying that precession might coincide with a revolution in spiritual thought. Even now, some are calling what we're entering, the Age of Light. The Golden Age."

I shook my head. "I'm sorry," I said, "but I'm just not seeing how all this is relevant." I remembered Rick's original description of Bill from their college days, and I had to wonder...for all his brilliance, was Bill just an aging hippie still on drugs?

He took my hand. "Jude, please, now, be patient with me."

"Ah, patience! Touché!" I laughed and took a deep breath. In my head I heard the monks from Varanasi counseling, *Listen. Suspend judgment. Be open. See for yourself.*

"I am still working this out," Bill was saying, "and I'm skeptical myself, but, well...my senses, my experiences... confirm that the world is in transition. Don't yours? The last fifty years have brought such drastic changes. In the future there will undoubtedly be even greater changes, and with them will come even greater stress. Our age is facing a grand challenge, which will necessarily have to move us beyond religious differences to solve our problems. We are desperate for a remarkable fuel invention, or at least remarkable alternatives, somewhat akin to what happened at the time of the industrial revolution. An invention, be it fusion or lassoing a star, is needed to replace our oil dependence if our planet is to continue thriving. We need sustainable clean energy."

"Well, sure," I said. "If we make it that long without annihilating ourselves."

He winked again, "True. How true. And there is apocalyptic literature from every age that would validate these concerns. But hold on, hold on. That is not our topic for the moment! I'm saying that climate change, energy source concerns, social unrest, religious rebooting, et cetera, are occurring simultaneously because they are part of a larger cycle influencing us. This is what I'm driving at, Jude: I think there is a global spirituality that is evolving along with, and in response to, the rest of these tremendous shifts, pressures, and cycles. I believe that a potential for a great and productive shift in the world's religious thinking is upon us. Perhaps the key ingredients that will transform the way we think are already in place. Perhaps we are at the threshold of a new view of God! So many people are fed up with the old views that don't work, don't answer the important questions, and only serve to divide us. Our time is ripe for spiritual change."

Just then, a car screeched around the corner of the parking garage. "Hey! Are you leaving?" The teenage driver leaned his whole upper body out the window and shouted over the booming bass of his stereo.

"Nope," I called out without turning around. "Sorry, not quite ready yet."

The car screeched off. Bill still held me in his bright blue stare.

"Well, Bill," I said slowly. "It's true that I have a new view of God. I feel as though I've made a great circle... and for me, like the ancient symbol itself, my circle is full of light. Full of Light." I repeated the word so he'd hear the capital L and understand what kind of light I meant. "I've come home, back to where I started, and everything is different. And everything is the same—"

"You have a feeling of completeness." He finished my sentence.

Yes, that's it. I feel a reassuring contentment from all I've discovered and all that I've been privileged to learn. I am a Jew, a Christian, a Hindu, a Muslim, a Buddhist, everything else, and nothing, all at once. I am. . .*whole*. If that makes any sense to you."

"It does," he said.

"And I believe that all religions possess and have knowledge of the Light. By claiming the Light myself, I can also retain my own personal stories, my own place, and time, and history and you know..."

Bill looked at me fondly. "It's the essence of spirituality, of our wholeness, to recognize that we are all united. That we are all of the same body. God is not a religion, does not speak a language and isn't a culture. Gods and names for God have changed throughout the ages. It is humans who attempt to make God static."

He paused. Suddenly we seemed to be at prayer

together, right there in a downtown parking garage. What an unlikely place. And how perfect it seemed.

"So you've had a taste of what life with the Light can be like," he said. "Now imagine if this knowledge were widespread. I've thought about nothing else since you began your journey." He numbered the changes on his fingers: "One. There would be no more religious wars. Two. No more ethnic fighting. Three. No more bombs in Jewish temples, Muslim mosques, or Christian churches. Four. No more genocide based on religious beliefs. Or racial stereotypes; for that matter. Muslims would not be against Christians, nor Jews against Muslims, Catholics against Protestants, Protestants against Jews. Buddhists would cease fighting Muslims, ditto Muslims and Hindus. And, five, groups like the Ku Klux Klan and the Neo-Nazis would have no reason to exist. Ah, I know it sounds like a dream. So much history of bloodshed and hatred. How do we heal that? If we lived the Light, taught it, shared it, I believe that within one or two generations the world might begin to experience freedom. And peace. Based not on the legends and myths of any one religion, but freedom finally because we honor something that is common to all as well as unique to each."

I had to think about this for a minute. Finally, "Oh, Bill, I don't know. All over the world I met people who seemed to feel the inklings of just what you're talking about. They even looked like you." I grinned and traced his silhouette in the air with my finger. "They were all... all shiny." He actually blushed. "But how can I say this? What you're describing is such a tall order, and if the knowledge of the Light has been around for so long, but we've never even come close to—"

He laid his hand on my shoulder, "Certainly it's a fantastic vision," he admitted. "But the world could use a *spiritual infusion,* just like we are desperate to save the environment."

The fierceness of his desire raced through me like a spark. "Whew," I said, and then I looked around the parking garage. "Umm, do you happen to remember where I parked my car?"

\* \* \*

The clatter of plates and silverware rattled through the house, a homey melody that had come to epitomize "Om Sweet Om" for me. For almost a year, my friends and I had been getting together to share a meal, and laughter, and the stories of the week before. We'd started small, just Gloria, Rick, Bill, and of course, John and me. But lately the group had been growing as other friends and friends of friends had caught wind of it.

But, well, I'm not telling the whole truth, the unveiled truth, shall we say. For we meet not just to eat and talk. We meet expressly to talk about the Light. How have we seen it? How have we expressed it in our daily lives? Or have we just been too preoccupied to notice it during the week just past? These are the questions that guide our conversation each week. Each of us has our own "practice."

I am, amazingly enough, still "sitting," still practicing my own slightly modified version of a light and sound meditation I learned in Varanasi. But I no longer expect to have a religious experience while I'm sitting on the cushion. Nor am I looking for one on the mountaintop, either literal or metaphorical. I'm just asking to stay open, to stay awake to all the revelations from the Light through the rest of my day.

In our little group, we have come to realize that we are mirrors for each other. And in the depth of our community, we have begun to dream and hope for breadth. Like Bill on that night when we had our long conversation in the parking garage, we have come to believe that we humans can achieve spiritual community on a global scale.

"Many beliefs, many stories, many legends—all ultimately resolved in one world spirit, one world Light." That's the way I put it, at least on hopeful days.

A familiar wail brings John and me running. The newest member of our group is miserable, and in this moment, our only job is to figure out why and what, if anything, we can do to help.

"Come here, darling," we both coo at once. "Jinx, you owe me," I add in an aside to John as I pick up our new baby. Lifting her high, I beam at her scrunched-up face. "What is it, sweetheart? What can we do for you?"

She wails again, and then gives a great belching hiccup. Our friends hear her, and conversation stops for just a moment.

Gabrielle opens her eyes and looks out on us.

And then, with a great shout of laughter, our friends go back to their eating and talking while John and I look down on our baby and at the Light that shines from her face.

Love and Light

Great things...
To live, to see, to experience,
the day that dawns,
the light that fills the world;
which fulfills our souls.

—Anonymous

# Postscript

This memoir, like many others, is a mix of fiction and fact. While most of this narrative is true, some sections were embellished for the reader's enjoyment. I was very fortunate to travel to nearly all of the destinations Jude visits.

# Glossary of Terms

*Akasha.* Sanskrit word meaning "aether." The record of the soul written in the realm of the Astral Light. It is possible to read the Akasha by spiritually attuning to that plane. In Hinduism, Akasha means the basis and essence of all things.

Akhenaten. Egyptian pharaoh who reigned approximately between 1360 and 1344 BCE. He is credited with giving the world its first monotheistic religion.

Alchemy. The art of transmutation. A traditional chemical philosophy having as its asserted aim the transmutation of base metals into gold, the discovery of the universal panacea, and the preparation of the elixir of longevity. Often used metaphorically to describe the purifying of the human soul.

*Alhamdulillah.* Arabic phrase meaning, "Praise to God."

Allah. The Arabic name for God to Muslims around the world.

*Amaterasu.* Amaterasu Omikami means the "Great Divinity Illuminating Heaven" and is the celestial sun goddess from whom the Japanese imperial family claims descent, and an important Shinto Deity.

*Amaterasu Omikami.* Shinto (Japanese) goddess of the sun. She carries a mirror.

*Ankhs.* A cross having a loop for its upper vertical arm. In ancient Egypt it served as an emblem of life.

*Ashram.* A usually secluded residence of a religious community and its guru.

*Aten.* Name of the monotheistic god of the Egyptian pharaoh Akhenaten.

BCE. Before the Common Era for years occurring before Year 1.

*Bhagavadgita.* Also spelled *Bhagavad Gita. The Song of Bhagavad.* A philosophical work that discusses the nature of consciousness, the self, the universe, and the Supreme.

*Canopic* jar. Egyptian funerary vessel in which was buried the embalmed internal organs removed from a body during the process of mummification.

Cayce, Edgar. Renowned 20th century American healer and psychic.

CE. Common Era for all dates starting with Year 1.

*Chakra.* From the Hindu, meaning a spinning wheel. Applied metaphysically to the human body as seven lighted centers of energy running down the midline of the body and said to correlate with the physical glands and spiritual energy of the individual.

Chanting. Spiritual tool, repetitive vocal practice. Because of its purpose and intent, chanting is interchangeable with prayer, meditation, or any other form that facilitates spiritual awareness.

Clear Light. Buddhist term designating the universal luminescence cultivated through serious spiritual practice.

*Djellaba.* Long gown or garment worn in Egypt.

DMT. N,N-Dimethyltryptamine is a psychedelic compound of the tryptamine family. Abbreviated as DMT and called the "spirit molecule." Naturally produced in the brain by the pineal gland and thought to give rise to paranormal experiences.

*Ein Sof.* The origin of "Infinite Light". May be translated as "no end" or "infinity".

*Felucca.* A traditional wooden sailboat used on the Nile River in Egypt. Also found elsewhere in the Mediterranean area.

*Ganesha.* Hindu god of wisdom and education. He looks like a well-dressed elephant.

*Ghats.* A series of steps leading down to a body of water, particularly a holy river such as the River Ganga in Varanasi.

God. When identified as "he," God refers to the male archetype (in Christianity, Jesus) or human image of the masculine aspect of divine energy. When used without gender association, God means the genderless indivisible energy made of both male

243

and female energy. An indivisible unit, androgynous in nature and without sexual distinction. The power that embraces and empowers within and without. Interchangeable with the Light.

Godhead. Highest or supreme power, both inner and outer, that embraces and empowers the universe. Interchangeable with the Light.

Golden mean. The middle between two extremes as stated by Aristotle and other philosophers. Can be applied to architecture, philosophy, and even politics.

*Hajj.* The annual pilgrimage to Mecca. One of the five Pillars of Faith in Islam.

*Hajji.* Muslim person who successfully completes the pilgrimage to Mecca.

*Hookah.* Sometimes called "hubbly-bubbly." A Middle Eastern tobacco pipe with a long flexible tube connected to a container in which the smoke is cooled by passing through water.

*Ishraq.* Arabic word meaning illumination.

*Itfaddal.* Means *please* in Arabic. Used when offering someone something.

Ka'bah. The building that is the holiest site in Islam and houses the mysterious Black Stone. From the Arabic word meaning cube or square house.

*Kabbalah.* Esoteric Kabbalah is a complete range of Jewish mystical activity which lays claim to secret knowledge of the unwritten Torah (divine revelation) that was communicated by God to Adam and Moses.

*Kali.* Hindu goddess of destruction, death, and regeneration.

*Kami.* Kami are the spirits or phenomena that are worshipped in Shinto and other indigenous religions of Japan. The term is often translated as "god," "mystical," or "divine" and means a deity or sacred power.

King Tut, or Tutankhamun. Egyptian boy pharaoh who became famous in the modern world after the discovery of his intact tomb in 1922. Said to have been Akhenaten's nephew, but recent DNA analysis confirms the boy king was Akhenaten's son.

*Lassi.* A refreshing drink from the Indian Subcontinent, which includes yogurt, water, spices, and sometimes fruit.

Light, the. A designation given to the undifferentiated godhead that appears as a radiant orb of luminescence and which feels like transcendental love to those who have experienced it. Not of this earthly world but found here. Other names include Supreme Luminescence, Mystic Light, the Divine Light, Living Burning Light, First Light, Primordial Light, Primary Light, and The Light. Also synonymous with Akhenaten's Aten and Moses' burning bush. In this work, the author often uses the term interchangeably with God and godhead.

Lucid dreaming. Becoming conscious in a dream that you are dreaming. Being awake and maintaining that awareness in your dream.

Macrocosm. The larger whole seen as a unit. The macrocosm is the sum total of the smaller subsystems that are contained within it. The reflection of the microcosm.

*Mani* stones. Rock faces or stone slabs that have Tibetan prayers carved on them.

Meditation. Spiritual practice and tool. Meditation is a listening state usually required to achieve awareness of the godhead.

*Menorah.* A seven-branched candelabra used in the religious rituals of Judaism.

*Merkabah* or *Merkavah.* A school of early Jewish mysticism.

Metaphysical. The deeper, often hidden, esoteric, and intrinsic meaning behind phenomena, religious practices, and spirituality.

Microcosm. The smaller sphere of activity and being. A system more or less analogous to the much larger system, or macrocosm, in its constitution, configuration, and development. Reflective of the macrocosm. The relationship of the macrocosm and the microcosm is said to be stated in the Hermetic axiom, "As above, so below."

Minaret. Part of the essential architecture of a mosque. The distinguishing feature that rises toward heaven. Similar to a church steeple.

Monstrance. A ceremonial vessel used during the Roman Catholic mass to display the consecrated communion host.

*Mundaka Upanishad.* Specific Vedic Sanskrit religious text having three parts and is among the most holy of all scriptures.

Nazarene. A native or inhabitant of Nazareth; Jesus. The title "Nazarene" may also have a religious significance instead of denoting a place of origin.

Near-death experience (NDE). The experience of a person who clinically dies but is revived and lives. NDEs are unique experiences occurring during near fatalities.

Occident. Western lands or regions; the West, precisely Europe.

*Om.* Hindu term for the eternal word or sound, often used as a mantra.

Orient. The divine location from which the Light first became manifest. The point of illumination. Also refers to the East (Asia) and the Near East.

Paradigm. An example or model. A consensus and agreement on a perceived pattern.

Pineal gland. A small, rudimentary, glandular body in the brain at the roof of the third ventricle, or approximately between the eyes in the forehead. Also called "pineal eye" or "pineal organ." Metaphysically believed to be the gland correlated with the sixth chakra or "third eye," which enables communication with the Divine. Newly discovered to produce DMT, the "spirit molecule" (see above). The pineal is the gland that Jesus was perhaps referring to when he said, "If thine eye be single, thy whole body will be filled with light."

Pituitary gland. An endocrine gland found attached to the base of the vertebrate brain. Its secretions, also involving the adjacent area called the hypothalamus, affect the other endocrine glands, so it is often considered the master gland of the body. Corresponds to the seventh chakra.

Precession. The cycle of the movement of the zodiac as one looks due east just before sunrise at the spring equinox. Nowadays, Pisces is seen. Depending on calculations, somewhere near 2650 CE we will have precessed to Aquarius. There is a strong feeling among metaphysicians that each approximately 2,000-year zodiac cycle influences earthly patterns. As we enter the Age of Aquarius, we will come under its dominion. The Age of Aquarius will be different from our current age, the Age of Pisces.

Qiblah. The direction, toward Mecca, a Muslim faces when he prays.

*Quais.* Arabic word meaning, " I am well or I am good."

*Quetzalcoatl.* Mesoamerican (Aztec) god, the Feathered Serpent. Some histories relate that the Aztecs identified the Spanish conquistadores as emissaries of Quetzalcoatl and welcomed them.

*Re* or *Ra.* Ancient Egyptian god whose symbol was the sun. Oldest deity in the ancient Egyptian pantheon.

Rosary. Beads used to recite and count a series of prayers on. Prayer tool used in the Catholic Church, but not uncommon in other religions for purposes of spiritual communion. Beads have been used in conjunction with a number of religious traditions such as Islam and initially in Hinduism.

Rosicrucians. Possibly medieval, possibly German, possibly invisible, possibly fictitious group that taught metaphysical and esoteric spiritual principles as possibly passed down from ancient Egypt. Also modern organizations based on medieval Rosicrucianism.

*Sadhu.* A Hindu holy man or ascetic.

*Sahtain.* Arabic word meaning double health. Spoken as one begins to take and enjoy food. Can also be spoken after the meal.

Saint Thecla of Ma'aluola. Also spelled Tekla and called Brikhta, which means Blessed. She is said to have witnessed the preaching of St. Paul and to have been the first Christian martyr exposed to wild animals.

*Samsara*. Sanskrit word used to describe birth, life, death, and the cycle of return.

*Scarab*. Important symbol in ancient Egyptian religion, in the form of the dung beetle. Associated with the divine manifestation of the early morning sun.

*Shari'a*. Islamic law, which regulates a Muslim's relationship with neighbors, the state, and with God.

*Shekinah*. Hebrew: "Dwelling" or "Presence".

*Shi'a*. Shi'a Islam is the smaller member of the two major branches of Islam representing approximately 15% of the total Muslim population. Shi'a followers believe that the proper succession of Islamic leadership after the death of Muhammad would have been Muhammad's cousin and son-in-law, Ali.

Shirley MacLaine. Oscar-winning actress, acclaimed dancer, singer, and best-selling author of metaphysical books. Born in 1934.

*Shiva*. Hindu god. Universal Creator and Destroyer of all things.

*Souk*. Open-air marketplace or commercial quarter in Middle Eastern cities.

Spontaneous human combustion. A rare phenomenon whereby a person is observed to catch fire.

*Sufi.* One who practices Sufism, which is the mystical dimension of Islam and is concerned with esoteric and metaphysical understanding of the divine.

*Sunni.* The larger member of the two major branches of Islam is the Sunni sect. They believed that the leader of the Islamic movement after the death of Muhammad should be elected. Abu Bakr, an advisor and close friend of Muhammad's was selected to be the leader or Caliph, upon the Prophet's death.

*Talmud.* The collection of ancient rabbinical writings consisting of the Mishnah and the Gemara and constituting the basis of religious authority in Orthodox Judaism.

Tantra. Hindu and Buddhist term designating a system that enables the practitioner to reach the godhead. Refers to the most elevated or highest spiritual practices.

*Tantric* yoga. Dealing with esoteric practices of some Hindu, Buddhist, and Jain sects.

*Torii* gate. Symbolic gateway marking the entrance to the sacred precincts of a Shinto shrine in Japan.

*Tuk tuk.* A three wheeled motorized vehicle common in India and Southeast Asia. Also known as an auto-rickshaw.

*Tumo.* The divine fire. Yogis capable of attaining *tumo* are able to control the internal energy systems of their bodies.

Transfiguration. An event recorded in the New Testament where Jesus is transfigured, or metamorphosed, and reveals himself to his disciples as a radiant being of Light. Described in Matthew 17:1–9, Mark 9:2–8, and Luke 9:28–36.

*Upanishads.* A collection of 200 Sanskrit texts containing many central religious concepts of Hinduism, some of which are shared with Buddhism and Jainism.

Venus. The planet seen from Earth as the evening and morning star. Associated with various divinities, primarily with love in mythology and astrology.

*Vishnu.* A god in the Hindu pantheon. "The Pervader," he is one of the three supreme deities.

*Vocatio.* From Latin meaning summons. Vocatio is a strong inclination to a particular state, a course of action, or a vocation.

Yin and Yang. Ancient Chinese concept and term denoting the feminine and masculine principles, essence, and nature. In the common circular symbol, each is impregnated with a seed of the other.

*Zoroastrianism.* Ancient religion founded by Zoroaster (or Zarathrustra) in Persia (present-day Iran) and dating back 3000+ years. Zoroaster sought to define life. Dualistic religion detailing the struggle between Light and Dark, or God and the Devil. Many Zoroastrian concepts have filtered into modern religions and today's dualistic thinking.

# Selected Bibliography

Aldred, Cyril. *Akhenaten: King of Egypt*. London: Thames and Hudson, Ltd., 1988.

Ali, Abdullah Yusuf. *Holy Koran*. American Trust Publications: 1997.

Alper, Matthew. *The "God" Part of the Brain: A Scientific Interpretation of Human Spirituality and God*. New York: Rogue Press, 2001.

Arden, Harvey. *In the Steps of Moses*. *National Geographic*: Washington, D.C., 1976.

Barrett, Matt. *Insight Guides India, 9th ed.* London: Apa Publications UK Ltd., 2011.

Berman, Phillip L. *The Journey Home: What Near-Death Experiences and Mysticism Teach Us about the Gift of Life*. New York: Pocket Books, Simon & Schuster, Inc., 1996.

Bharati, Agehananda. *The Light at the Center: Context and Pretext of Modern Mysticism*. Santa Barbara: Ross-Erickson, 1976.

Breasted, James Henry. *Development of Religion and Thought in Ancient Egypt*. New York: Harper and Row, 1959.

Brewer, E. Cobham. *A Dictionary of Miracles: Imitative, Realistic, and Dogmatic*. New York: J. B. Lippincott, 1966.

Catholic Biblical Association of America. *The New American Bible*. New York: Thomas Nelson, 1983.

Choegyal, Lisa. *Insight Guides Nepal*, 1st ed. London: Apa Publications UK Ltd., 1991.

David, A. Rosalie. *The Ancient Egyptians: Beliefs and Practices*. London: Routledge and Kegan Paul, Ltd., 1982.

Dowell, W. "A Crag Where Aramaic Lives," *Time International*, Oct. 1989.

Eadie, Betty. *Embraced by the Light*. Placerville, CA: Gold Leaf Press, 1992.

Eliade, Mircea. *Encyclopedia of Religion*. Chicago: University of Chicago Press, 1988.

_____. *The Two and the One*. Chicago: University of Chicago Press, 1979.

Fadiman, Dorothy. *Light: Its Spiritual Aspects*. Hartley Film Foundation: Michael Wiese. 1978.

Freud, Sigmund. *Moses and Monotheism*. New York: Vintage Books, 1939.

Gairdner, W.H.T. *Al-Ghazzali's Mishkat Al-Anwar: The Niche for Lights*. Lahore, Pakistan: Muhammad Ashraf, 1960.

Haraldsson, Erlendur and Karlis Osis. *At the Hour of Death: A New Look at Evidence for Life After Death*. New York: Avon Books, 1977.

Israel, Samuel and Bikram Grewal. *Insight Guides Rajasthan, India,* 1st ed. Apa Publications HK Ltd., 1989.

Jung, Carl G.. *Man and His Symbols*. New York: Dell Publishing, 1968.

Kelzer, Kenneth. The Sun and the Shadow. Virginia Beach: A.R.E. Press, 1987.

Klein, H. Arthur. *Bioluminescence*. New York: J. B. Lippincott, 1965.

_____. *Masers and Lasers*. New York: J. B. Lippincott, 1969.

Kübler-Ross, Elizabeth. *On Death and Dying*. New York: Touchstone, 1969.

LaBerge, Stephen. *Lucid Dreaming*. Los Angeles: Jeremy P. Tarcher, 1985.

Lehner, Mark. *The Egyptian Heritage: Based on the Edgar Cayce Readings*. Virginia Beach: A.R.E Press, 1974.

Luce, Gay Gaer. *Body Time*. New York: Pantheon Books, 1971.

Lurker, Manfred. *The Gods and Symbols of Ancient Egypt*. London: Thames and Hudson, 1974.

McGarey, William. *Light, Healing, and Consciousness. Venture Inward*. Virginia Beach: A.R.E. Press, July/August 1989.

Miller, M.S. and J. Lane Miller. *Black's Bible Dictionary*. New York: Harper and Row, 1961.

Moody, Raymond. *Life After Life: The Investigation of a Phenomenon—Survival of Bodily Death.*. New York: Bantam Books, 1975.

Morse, Melvin and Paul Perry. *Closer to the Light: Learning from the Near-Death Experiences of Children*. New York: Ivy Books, 1990.

Morris, R. *Light*. New York: Bobbs-Merrill Inc., 1973.

Nicholson, Louise. *National Geographic Traveler: India*, 2nd ed. *National Geographic*. Washington, D.C., 2001.

Ott, John N. *Health and Light*. New York: Pocket Books, 1976.

Randle, Kevin D. *To Touch the Light*. New York: Windsor Publishing Corp., 1994.

Sargeant, Winthrop. *Bhagavad Gita*. New York: Doubleday, 1979.

Singh, Sarina. *Lonely Planet: India, 11th ed.* Australia: Lonely Planet Publications Pty Ltd., 2005.

Sparrow, G. Scott. *Lucid Dreaming: Dawning of the Clear Light.* Virginia Beach: A.R.E. Press, 1976.

Staal, Frits. *Exploring Mysticism: An Anthropological Essay.* Berkeley: University of California Press, 1975.

Strassman, Rick MD. *DMT: The Spirit Molecule: A Doctor's Revolutionary Research into the Biology of Near-Death and Mystical Experiences.* Rochester, VT: Park Street Press, 2001.

Weigall, Arthur E. P. *The Life and Times of Akhnaton: Pharaoh of Egypt.* Edinburgh and London: William Blackwood and Sons, 1910.

# About the Author

JUDITH T. LAMBERT (*www.judithtlambertbooks.com*) commutes between worlds. For 35 years, she has divided her time between communities in the Kingdom of Saudi Arabia, Thailand, and the USA. Judith holds a master's degree in religious studies from John F. Kennedy University in Orinda, California. Extensive travels have enabled her to deepen her study of cultures and religions firsthand. She lives with her husband, John, and their daughter, Gabrielle. Her other books include *A Mother Goddess for Our Times: Mary's Appearances at Medjugorje* and *Gabrielle's Magical Pets*, a picture book illustrated by her daughter.

Made in the USA
Columbia, SC
22 June 2017